God's Wisdom

Making HIM Known

God's Names
God's Promise
God's Providence
God's Wisdom

God's Wisdom

BY SALLY MICHAEL

P&R
PUBLISHING
P.O. BOX 817 • PHILLIPSBURG • NEW JERSEY 08865-0817

© 2014 text by Next Generation Resources, Inc., illustrations by Fred Apps

All rights reserved. No part of this book may be reproduced, stored in a retrieval system, or transmitted in any form or by any means—electronic, mechanical, photocopy, recording, or otherwise—except for brief quotations for the purpose of review or comment, without the prior permission of the publisher, P&R Publishing Company, P.O. Box 817, Phillipsburg, New Jersey 08865-0817.

Unless otherwise indicated, Scripture quotations are from *ESV Bible* ® (*The Holy Bible, English Standard Version* ®). Copyright © 2001 by Crossway Bibles, a publishing ministry of Good News Publishers. Used by permission. All rights reserved.

Scripture quotations marked (NIV) are from the HOLY BIBLE, NEW INTERNATIONAL VERSION®. NIV®. Copyright © 1973, 1978, 1984 by International Bible Society. Used by permission of Zondervan Publishing House. All rights reserved.

ISBN: 978-1-59638-862-8 (pbk)
ISBN: 978-1-59638-863-5 (ePub)
ISBN: 978-1-59638-864-2 (Mobi)

Page design and typesetting by Dawn Premako

Printed in the United States of America

Library of Congress Cataloging-in-Publication Data

Michael, Sally, 1953-
  God's wisdom / by Sally Michael. -- 1st [edition].
    pages cm
  Includes bibliographical references.
  ISBN 978-1-59638-862-8 (pbk.)
 1. Wisdom--Biblical teaching. 2. Bible--Study and teaching. 3. Bible. Proverbs--Criticism, interpretation, etc. 4. Christian education of children. I. Title.
  BS680.W6M43 2014
  223'.706--dc23

                            2013031310

Dedicated to
David Glenn House.

May you walk in God's wisdom
all the days of your life
and follow Jesus
on the path that leads to life.

Blessed is the one who finds wisdom,
and the one who gets understanding,
for the gain from her is better than gain from silver
and her profit better than gold.
She is more precious than jewels,
and nothing you desire can compare with her.
Long life is in her right hand;
in her left hand are riches and honor.
Her ways are ways of pleasantness,
and all her paths are peace.
She is a tree of life to those who lay hold of her;
those who hold her fast are called blessed.
—Proverbs 3:13–18

Contents

Preface 9

Introduction: How to Use This Book 12

1. Jesus Is the Sure Foundation 16
2. Two Paths 20
3. Wisdom and Foolishness 24
4. Wisdom Is a Treasure 28
5. Run from Foolishness 32
6. The Mocking Fool 36
7. The Rebellious Fool 40
8. The Godless Fool 44
9. The Simple Fool 48
10. Foolishness Leads to Destruction 52
11. Driving Out Folly 56
12. Get Wisdom 60
13. Fearing God: Who He Is 64
14. Fearing God: What He Is Like—Perfect in Everything 68
15. Fearing God: What He Is Like—Amazing Love 72

16. Imitating God 76

17. The Wise Seek Knowledge 80

18. The Wise Love God's Commands 84

19. The Wise Hate Evil 88

20. The Wise Listen to Advice 92

21. The Wise Accept Correction 96

22. The Wise Have Self-Control 100

23. The Wise Look Ahead 104

24. The Wise Trust God 108

25. The End of the Path 112

26. Jesus Is the Bridge 116

Preface

How much better to get wisdom than gold!
To get understanding is to be chosen rather than silver.
—Proverbs 16:16

What a beautiful picture of wisdom is painted in the book of Proverbs! Wisdom is a great treasure; more precious than jewels and more profitable to the human soul than silver or gold. Yet in spite of the beauty and value of wisdom, the human heart is naturally bent toward foolishness due to our sin nature inherited from our father Adam. How we need the work of Christ on the cross to subdue our sin nature and set our feet on the path of wisdom!

Every day our children are confronted with the call of wisdom and the call of foolishness. Which call will they answer? Will they be attracted to the foolishness of rebellion against God and His ways? Or will they embrace Christ and understand the wisdom and protection of God's commands? Will they willfully follow the course of this world and shut God out of their lives? Or will they come to fear the Lord and hate evil? Will they stubbornly insist on following their own counsel? Or will they humbly listen to advice and accept correction? Will they blindly follow their sinful urges? Or will they exhibit self-control and look ahead to the consequences of their choices and actions? Which path will our children travel through life—the life-giving path of wisdom or the destructive path of foolishness?

Our children are born on the path of foolishness, naturally inclined to resist loving what is good and right (Proverbs 22:15). With their natural attraction toward foolishness, how will they learn to treasure wisdom, follow its counsel, and walk in the way of the wise?

Loving wisdom and what is good and right begins with the work of God in the heart. The desire and strength to reject the path of foolishness comes from knowing God, who is the source of wisdom. When God inclines a child's heart to be in awe of His greatness and goodness, the result is the fear of the Lord, which is the beginning of wisdom.

> The fear of the Lord is the beginning of wisdom,
>   and the knowledge of the Holy One is insight. (Proverbs 9:10)

Only Jesus is the bridge from the path of foolishness to the path of wisdom. When children embrace Jesus, the Light in a dark world, they will begin to treasure wisdom and walk in its ways.

You have been given the high calling of introducing your child to Jesus Christ and imparting the words of life-giving wisdom. May you and your child discover together the joys of wisdom and the destruction of foolishness in the pages of this book, which is based on the Book of all books, God's Holy Word. May your authentic example of trusting God, and your diligent instruction of His character and His ways, incline your child's heart to love the way of wisdom. And may the glimpses of our great and glorious God draw your child to fear the Lord and walk in all His ways.

> My son, be attentive to my words;
>   incline your ear to my sayings.
> Let them not escape from your sight;
>   keep them within your heart.
> For they are life to those who find them,
>   and healing to all their flesh.
> Keep your heart with all vigilance,
>   for from it flow the springs of life.
> Put away from you crooked speech,
>   and put devious talk far from you.

Let your eyes look directly forward,
    and your gaze be straight before you.
Ponder the path of your feet;
    then all your ways will be sure.
Do not swerve to the right or to the left;
    turn your foot away from evil. (Proverbs 4:20–27)

My son, keep your father's commandment,
    and forsake not your mother's teaching.
Bind them on your heart always;
    tie them around your neck.
When you walk, they will lead you;
    when you lie down, they will watch over you;
    and when you awake, they will talk with you.
For the commandment is a lamp and the teaching a light,
    and the reproofs of discipline are the way of life. (Proverbs 6:20–23)

Introduction
How to Use This Book

This book was written to give parents an opportunity to present solid truth to their children and to encourage real-life application of that truth.

Relational

Children receive more encouragement to learn when truth is presented by a trusted individual. Your positive, relational parent-child commitment will be a real benefit when you sit down together to read this book. Your time together over the Word should be positive, affirming, and loving.

Interactive

There is a greater impact when an individual *discovers* truth instead of just hearing it presented. Many questions have been incorporated into the text of this book to encourage your child to wonder and think critically. The process of discovery will be circumvented if you don't give your child adequate time to think and respond. After asking a question, wait for a response. If your child has difficulty, ask the question in a different way or give a few hints.

Questions and responses can be springboards for more questions and discovery as you interact with your child's mind and heart. The Holy Spirit is the real teacher, so depend on Him to give both you and your child thoughts and truths to explore together, and to bring the necessary understanding. Take the time to work through each story at a leisurely pace—giving time for interaction and further dialogue. The goal should be to get the material into the child, not just to get the child through the material.

Understandable

These stories have been written with attention given to explaining difficult or potentially new concepts. Some of these concepts may take time for your child to digest. Allow your child to ponder new truths. Read the story more than once, allowing the truth to be better understood and integrated into your child's theological framework. At times, have your child read parts of the lesson, giving an opportunity for visual learning.

Because vocabulary can be child-specific, define the particular words foreign to your child. Retell difficult sections in familiar wording, and ask questions to be sure your child understands the truth being taught.

Theological

More than just acquainting your child with an understanding of wisdom, this book is building a foundation of biblical theology for your child. As your child begins to correctly understand who God is and the wisdom of His ways, he or she won't just have a vague notion of God, but will be able to relate to the God of the Bible.

Because the Word of God has convicting and converting power, Bible texts are quoted word for word in some parts. Some of these verses may be beyond the child's understanding, so you may want to explain unfamiliar words or thoughts. Even though clear comprehension may be difficult, hearing the Word itself is a means that the Holy Spirit often uses to encourage faith in your child (Romans 10:17). Do not minimize the effectual influence of God's Word in the tender souls of children.

Since the Word of God is living and active, allow the child to read the actual Bible verses as much as possible. Also, encourage your child to memorize some of the verses so he or she can meditate on them at other times.

The gospel is presented numerous times throughout the book. Use this as an opportunity to share God's work of grace in your life, and to converse with your child about his or her spiritual condition. Be careful not to confuse spiritual interest with converting faith, and take care to avoid giving premature assurances. Fan the flames of gospel-inspired conviction and tenderness toward the sacrificial love of Jesus without prematurely encouraging your child to pray "the sinner's prayer."[1]

Application

Understanding the truth is essential, but understanding alone is insufficient. Truth must also be embraced in the heart and acted upon in daily life. Often, children cannot make the connection between a biblical truth and real-life application, so you, the parent, must help bridge the gap.

Consider the following quotation by Dr. Martyn Lloyd-Jones:

> We must always put things in the right order, and it is Truth first. . . . The heart is always to be influenced through the understanding—the mind, then the heart, then the will. . . . But God forbid that anyone should think that it ends with the intellect. It starts there, but it goes on. It then moves the heart and finally the man yields his will. He obeys, not grudgingly or unwillingly, but with the whole heart. The Christian life is a glorious perfect life that takes up and captivates the entire personality.[2]

Spend a few days or even a week on each story. Reread the story, discuss the truths, and follow the suggestions in the Learning to Trust God section. Most importantly, help your child to see that God is who He says He is, and help him or her to act in response to the truth. Point out God's involvement in daily life,

---

1. Some excellent resources for parents regarding the salvation of children can be found at www.childrendesiringgod.org, including a booklet titled *Helping Children to Understand the Gospel* and two seminars from the 2007 Children Desiring God conference, How Great a Salvation—"Leading Children to a Solid Faith" and "Presenting the Gospel to Children."

2. D. Martyn Lloyd-Jones, *Spiritual Depression* (Grand Rapids: William B. Eerdmans, 1965), 61–62.

thank Him for being true to His Word, and ask him to grant us a measure of His wisdom as we seek to walk and live in his ways.

Prayer

Ultimately, our efforts are effective only if the Holy Spirit breathes on our teaching and quickens it to the heart. Pray not only before going through the stories, but also in the succeeding days, that your child would see God's character expressed in His Word, learn to live by His wisdom, and respond to Him in faith.

Jesus Is the Sure Foundation

Suppose you want to build a house from blocks. You can't just build the house in the air. You have to build it on something, on a foundation. Would it be better to build your house on a table, or on a ball? Why?

It would be very foolish to build your house on a ball, wouldn't it? Even if you built the house well, just one small roll of the ball could make the house tumble down. But a table is strong and stable. It is a good foundation for a house of blocks.

Jesus told a story about two men who built houses and the foundations they used. One man was wise and built his house on a rock foundation. The other was foolish and built his house on the sand. Do you know what happened to the two houses when the rain came and the wind blew? The house on the rock stood firm. But the house on the sand "fell, and great was the fall of it" (Matthew 7:24–27).

Would you rather be like the wise man or the foolish man? Jesus said wise people are those who hear His words and put them into practice. They are like the man who built his house on a rock. They have a sure, strong foundation for life. But those who hear the Word of God and do not practice it—do not obey it—are foolish like the man who built his house on the sand. Their foundation isn't good. It's shaky and weak, and someday they will fall with a great crash.

Adam and Eve had a good foundation. They had a relationship with the living God. They walked and talked with Him. He gave them all they needed. He was their Creator, Protector, and Provider. He was also their Ruler, telling them to live in obedience to Him. God was the solid, sure, strong foundation for Adam and Eve.

But they were like the foolish man who hears the Word of God and does not practice it. They chose to step off the sure foundation of trusting God, and they disobeyed God and turned away from His rule. They foolishly chose the sandy foundation of sin, selfishness, pride, and disobedience. And "great was the fall" of Adam and Eve . . . and of all people because

> by the one man's disobedience the many were made sinners. (Romans 5:19)

Adam's disobedience brought sin into the world, and those born after him were born in sin.[1] Here is one way to understand this:

> Cows have baby . . . cows.
> Dogs have baby . . . dogs.
> Sinners have baby . . . sinners.

---

1. With the exception of Jesus.

Horses are never born to cows, and cats are never born to dogs. Cows have baby cows, horses have baby horses. So sinners have baby sinners. Just like "cow-ness" or "cow nature" is passed on from the mother and father cow to the baby, so sin nature is passed on from Adam and Eve to their children, who pass it on to their children, who pass it on to their children . . . to us. So we are born with a sin nature. We are born on a shaky foundation of pride, selfishness, and disobedience—a foundation of sin.

But God made a way of rescue from the sandy foundation.

> For as by the one man's disobedience the many were made sinners, so by the one man's obedience the many will be made righteous. (Romans 5:19)

Just as sin came through one man, Adam, rescue from sin and foolishness and a sandy foundation came through one man—one man who obeyed God perfectly, had no sin, paid the price for foolishness and disobedience, and died for undeserving sinners. Do you know who that man is?

He is Jesus, the sinless, perfect Son of God. Jesus died on the cross to take the punishment for sin, to rescue man from his foolish, sinful heart, and to place those who trust in Him on a strong, sure foundation. Through one man came sin, and through one man, Jesus, came salvation from sin.

People build their lives on all kinds of foundations. Their foundations are the things they trust in—like money, friendships, good looks, possessions, or abilities like being good at sports or music. These are shaky, sandy foundations. When the rains of problems and the winds of death come, these foundations wash away. They can't last.

But there is one foundation that is solid and will not wash away. That foundation can stand the rains of problems and the winds of death. It is a sure, strong, solid foundation, and it is the *only* sure, strong, solid foundation for life.

> For no one can lay a foundation other than that which is laid, which is Jesus Christ. (1 Corinthians 3:11)

Trusting in Jesus is the sure foundation for rescue from sin and the power to live in obedience to God, practicing His Word. Wise people build their lives trusting in Jesus; foolish people grab on to sandy foundations. What is your foundation? Do you want to be wise or foolish?

LEARNING TO TRUST GOD

✣ Read the story of the wise man and the foolish man in Matthew 7:24–27. Is just knowing about God enough to save you? What are some of the "words of mine" that Jesus talked about?

✣ Read Philippians 3:3–9. What are the two foundations Paul talks about in these verses? What is the difference between these foundations? What is "faith in Christ"?

✣ *Activity:* Try building something on different kinds of foundations. How important is the foundation? As a family, think of a way you can tell someone about the sure foundation of faith in Jesus and then follow through this week (e.g., tell them the gospel story, show them a movie with a gospel message, write a note, etc.).

Two Paths

Have you ever been hiking? Did you have to choose between two different paths? What if one was rocky, narrow, and uphill, and the other was wide, flat, and easy to travel? Which would most people choose? Which would you choose? What if you knew the narrow, hard path led to a beautiful castle and the wide, easy path led to a smelly garbage dump?

Life is like that. There are two paths you can travel, each going to a different place. This is what the Bible tells us about these two different ways through life:

> Enter by the narrow gate. For the gate is wide and the way is easy that leads to destruction, and those who enter by it are many. For the gate is narrow and the way is hard that leads to life, and those who find it are few. (Matthew 7:13–14)

One path has a narrow gate and the way is hard . . . but it leads to eternal life in heaven. The other has a wide gate and the way is very easy . . . but it leads to destruction in hell. The narrow, hard path is called the way of the wise, and the wide, easy path is called the way of the foolish. Few travel the narrow, hard path to heaven, but many travel the wide, easy path to hell. Why is that?

People in the days of Noah were walking on the wide path of foolishness. They took the easy path of doing whatever their evil hearts wanted. They did not fight sin or have faith in God. They did not do what is right or think about the end of their path of foolishness. So God sent Noah to warn them. Noah preached about the sure foundation of faith in God and way of wisdom.[1]

---

1. Although the Genesis 6 account does not say that Noah preached to the people, 2 Peter 2:5 calls him a "herald of righteousness." Given this, we surmise that Noah must have preached to his fellow men while building the ark.

But the people didn't listen. They kept on the way of foolishness and destruction. Their easy path of foolishness led to a flood, but even more, it ended in destruction—not just the destruction of their lives in the flood, but also the eternal destruction of their souls in hell. But Noah and his family were saved. Noah chose the way of wisdom, the way to life on earth after the flood and life in heaven forever.

The foolish people of Noah's day did not hear and obey the Word of God. They ignored God's warning—and they were destroyed.

When a fire alarm goes off, what should you do? A fire alarm is a warning. It tells us that there is danger—a fire that could kill you. Foolish people ignore fire alarms, but wise people obey them and run from the fire.

The Bible has a warning for all of us about a fire to come—an eternal fire, everlasting death, and destruction. The foolish will ignore this warning. But the wise will listen and obey. The book of Proverbs has many of these warnings from God and teachings about the way of the wise. It tells us to follow the way of wisdom and run from the way of the foolish:

> I have taught you the way of wisdom;
>   I have led you in the paths of uprightness.
> When you walk, your step will not be hampered,
>   and if you run, you will not stumble.
> Keep hold of instruction; do not let go;
>   guard her, for she is your life.
> Do not enter the path of the wicked,
>   and do not walk in the way of the evil.
> Avoid it; do not go on it;
>   turn away from it and pass on. (Proverbs 4:11–15)

What does this tell you about the teaching of the Bible? It tells you to grab on to it—love and follow it—because it will protect you and lead to eternal life. God's Word is full of instruction, teaching us about the way of the wise, the way of faith, the way to eternal life. Listening to and obeying the Bible is taking the narrow path that leads to life.

What is the warning in these verses? The Bible tells us to not even enter the path of the wicked—don't even set a foot on the way of foolishness. Keep away from it, pass by it, run from it. This is a good warning. It is like a fire alarm warning you of danger and destruction. But you must choose to listen.

What path will you follow: The way of wisdom, trusting and obeying God, or the way of foolishness? The path of safety and life, or the way of destruction and death? The way of holiness, or the way of sin? What joy there is for those who choose the way of the wise!

And a highway shall be there,
    and it shall be called the Way of Holiness;
the unclean shall not pass over it.
    It shall belong to those who walk on the way;
    even if they are fools, they shall not go astray.
No lion shall be there,
    nor shall any ravenous beast come up on it;
they shall not be found there,
    but the redeemed shall walk there.
And the ransomed of the Lord shall return
    and come to Zion with singing;
everlasting joy shall be upon their heads;
    they shall obtain gladness and joy,
    and sorrow and sighing shall flee away. (Isaiah 35:8–10)

LEARNING TO TRUST GOD

✢ Read Genesis 6. Why did God send the flood? How do we know that Noah was following the way of the wise?

✢ Read Isaiah 35:8–10 again. What is the Way of Holiness like, and what is its end? Ask God to give you a heart to follow the path that leads to life.

✢ *Activity:* Take a hike with your family and listen to the instruction of your father and mother. How can you guard this instruction? How are you tempted to follow the path of the wicked? How can you run from this path?

Wisdom and Foolishness

What do you love? Candy? Pizza? Those are just things you *like* a lot. What do you really *love*? What is really important to you? Besides your family, what else would you say? Do you love generosity, kindness, and truth? Or do you love getting your own way and making sure you always get the best?

What you love will determine what you do. If you love generosity, you will cheerfully share with others. If you love yourself, you will selfishly guard what is yours. If you love work and responsibility, you will eagerly do your chores and homework. If you love play, you will complain and put off doing your work. To know what you love, look at what you do when you have a choice.

So what do you really *love*? The true answer will show whether you are wise or foolish. Wise people love what is right and good, and do those things. Wisdom is not just *knowing* what is right. It is *doing* what is right because you love what is right and good. It is *loving* kindness, generosity, telling the truth, and treating people fairly—and *doing* those things.

What is foolishness? Foolishness is loving what is wrong and bad and doing it. It is following the wide, easy path that leads to destruction. There are two paths through life—the wise and the foolish. What you love will control which path you follow.

The people in the church of Macedonia followed the path of wisdom—they loved what is right and good. They were wise, loving generosity and acting in generous ways. They were very poor, but they knew that the Christians in Jerusalem needed help. So they generously gave the little they had. Why did they do that?

No one forced them to be generous. They did it on their own and were really happy to help. They had "overflowing joy" that they could give to others.

Their abundance of joy and their extreme poverty have overflowed in a wealth of generosity on their part. (2 Corinthians 8:2)

Why did they give so much? They loved God, and they loved what He loves. They loved what is good and right. Their hearts were so full of loving generosity that they were happy to share what they had. They *wanted* to be generous. What a joyful way to live!

The Bible also tells us about some foolish people—Ananias and Sapphira from Jerusalem.

Just as in Macedonia, the Christians in Jerusalem loved and did what is good and right. They were generous because they loved God, and they made sure everyone had what they needed. Sometimes they sold land or houses and brought the money to the apostles—the church leaders—to give to people who needed help. They were walking in the way of wisdom—loving generosity and kindness, caring for others, and doing what is good and right.

Ananias and his wife, Sapphira, sold some land. They decided to give some of the money to the apostles to help others. That was good. What was not good was that they also decided to pretend that the money they were giving away was *all* the money they had got for the land.

When Ananias brought the money to the apostles, Peter said,

> Ananias, why has Satan filled your heart to lie to the Holy Spirit and to keep back for yourself part of the proceeds of the land? While it remained unsold, did it not remain your own? And after it was sold, was it not at your disposal? Why is it that you have contrived this deed in your heart? You have not lied to men but to God. (Acts 5:3–4)

What was in Ananias' heart? Pride? Dishonesty? He pretended to be more generous than he really was. He did not love the truth. He did not love wisdom and walking in the way of the wise. He was foolish, loving and doing what is wrong and bad.

What happened to Ananias? He fell down and died! His foolish sin led to destruction.

Sapphira also followed the path of foolishness. She, too, lied about the money to the apostles . . . and she fell down dead like her husband. What sadness the way of foolishness brings![1]

Will you follow the way of the wise like the church in Macedonia? Or the way of the foolish like Ananias and Sapphira? What do you love? Only Jesus can give you a heart to love what is good and right. What you love will guide your feet to the path you choose.

---

1. Instantly falling down dead is an unusual consequence to foolishness, but foolishness always brings some kind of consequence.

> For no good tree bears bad fruit, nor again does a bad tree bear good fruit, for each tree is known by its own fruit. For figs are not gathered from thornbushes, nor are grapes picked from a bramble bush. The good person out of the good treasure of his heart produces good, and the evil person out of his evil treasure produces evil, for out of the abundance of the heart his mouth speaks. (Luke 6:43–45)

LEARNING TO TRUST GOD

- Read Luke 6:43–45 again. How does the lesson about trees and fruit help us understand our hearts and actions? Can you change your heart? What can you do to help your heart?

- Read Acts 4:32–5:11. What does *"contrived this deed in your heart"* mean? What is the connection between Ananias' heart and his actions? Name some actions and heart attitudes that are foolish and some that are wise. What is the difference between doing a foolish action and following the way of foolishness? Between doing a wise action and following the way of wisdom?

- *Activity:* Have each family member tell about one wise and one foolish action he or she did this week. What were the heart attitudes behind each? Make a reminder card of the definitions of wisdom and foolishness (loving what is _____ and doing it). Pray for a wise heart for each other. Then perform a kind deed for someone.[2]

---

2. Note: Though a kind deed can be done with a wrong heart, it is also true that doing what is right will sometimes help to shape the attitudes of the heart. Continue to pray for a wise heart that loves and does what is good and right for one another.

Wisdom Is a Treasure

Tales of buried treasure are so exciting! Don't you wish you had a treasure map to lead you to a hidden chest of riches?

Well, in a way you do! The Bible says that wisdom is a treasure—better than gold or silver, more precious than jewels!

> Blessed is the one who finds wisdom,
>   and the one who gets understanding,
> for the gain from her is better than gain from silver
>   and her profit better than gold.
> She is more precious than jewels,
>   and nothing you desire can compare with her. (Proverbs 3:13–15)

If you knew a treasure was hidden in your backyard, what would you do? You would look for it! You would get a shovel and dig, turning over every rock and looking under every bush until you found it.

Well, wisdom is a treasure—and we need to dig to find it. We need to look for it with all our might.

> The beginning of wisdom is this: Get wisdom,
>   and whatever you get, get insight. (Proverbs 4:7)

So where do we look for wisdom? We look to the One who created wisdom and has all wisdom—God. In His words in the Bible, we find what is good and right, and we find the heart to do what is good and right.

Do you know which book of the Bible tells us a lot about wisdom? The book of Proverbs. Proverbs are wise sayings that show us what is right to do. The teaching in Proverbs helps us understand how to act in a godly way, how to make decisions, and how to know what is best. But even more than that, Proverbs shows us why God's way is best so that we will have a heart to walk in God's way, which is the way of the wise.

Do you know any proverbs from the Bible? What are some of your favorites? How about:

> A joyful heart is good medicine,
> but a crushed spirit dries up the bones. (Proverbs 17:22)

A joyful heart makes everyone feel better. It is good medicine. But crabbiness upsets everyone. It is unpleasant and dries up the bones. This is a wise saying—it shows us how to live right.

> A soft answer turns away wrath,
> but a harsh word stirs up anger. (Proverbs 15:1)

Speaking a kind word to an angry person can help him calm down and not be so angry. But saying something mean only makes him angrier. Can you see why God's ways are best?

Here is some more good advice about our words from the book of Proverbs:

> Gracious words are like a honeycomb,
>   sweetness to the soul and health to the body. (Proverbs 16:24)

This verse tells us to say gracious or kind words. They are sweet to people—like honey is sweet. But being wise is not just *knowing* what is good and right to do. A truly wise person *does* what is good and right because he *loves* what is good and right. The wise person doesn't just know gracious words; he speaks gracious words. He has a heart that wants to follow God's way, the way of wisdom.

The book of Proverbs calls these words of wisdom, these wise sayings, a chain.

> Listen, my son, to your father's instruction,
>   and do not forsake your mother's teaching.
> They will be a garland to grace your head
>   and a chain to adorn your neck. (Proverbs 1:8–9 NIV)

What kind of chain is Proverbs talking about—a heavy chain that holds you tight and forces you to follow the way of wisdom, or a beautiful chain necklace, something you want and like? A chain that "adorns your neck" is a necklace that looks beautiful and brings beauty to you. Wisdom is like a special necklace that makes a person beautiful and happy.

Do you know what a garland is? A garland is a beautiful wreath of flowers. Just like a garland of flowers, wisdom is beautiful. It is a great treasure. Walking in the way of the wise, loving what is good and right and doing it, brings true joy.

If you love Jesus and are trusting in His ways, obeying the way of wisdom is a happy, beautiful thing, and not an awful "have to" thing. Do you love what is good and right? Do you have joy in doing what is wise? Do you look for wisdom? Are you eager to learn to follow God's ways? Knowing the way of wisdom, what is good and right, can be found in God's Word . . . and God can give you love for what is good and right as you read about His ways in His Word.

Blessed is the one who finds wisdom,
> *and the one who gets understanding,*
for the gain from her is better than gain from silver
> *and her profit better than gold.*
She is more precious than jewels,
> *and nothing you desire can compare with her. (Proverbs 3:13–15)*

LEARNING TO TRUST GOD

✤ Read Proverbs 1. Why was Proverbs written?

✤ Read Proverbs 1:8–9 again. Does your parents' teaching feel like a heavy chain or a beautiful necklace? Are you eager to learn about what is good and right and to obey the good teaching of your parents from the Bible?

✤ *Activity:* Copy some verses from Proverbs on separate pieces of paper and hide them around the house for your family to find this week. Each one is a treasure. When you find a verse, think about what it means and how you can act on the verse. At the end of the week, share with each other the verses you found and how you acted on them. Why is the wisdom of these verses a treasure to love? Have a special treat as a reminder that wisdom is precious, beautiful, and pleasant.

Run from Foolishness

When someone calls out to you, what does he want you to do? Usually he wants you to pay attention and listen to what he has to say.

Did you know that wisdom calls out to you every day, too, and wants you to listen?

> Wisdom cries aloud in the street,
>   in the markets she raises her voice;
> at the head of the noisy streets she cries out;
>   at the entrance of the city gates she speaks. (Proverbs 1:20–21)

The wise words of the Bible call out to get our attention, to get us to listen, and to get us to love them and obey. When you read a verse in the Bible that shows you what is good and right, that is wisdom calling to you. When God gives you a thought about something good to do, wisdom is calling. Wisdom is calling when your father gives you good advice.

But wisdom is not the only one calling to us. Foolishness calls out to us, too. Do you remember what foolishness is? It is not just being silly—like when you put socks on your hands or make funny faces. Foolishness is having your heart in the wrong place. It is loving what is wrong and bad, and obeying the call to do those wrong and bad things.

Foolishness is loving selfishness, unkindness, laziness, and all sorts of wrong and bad things. And since we most often follow what we love, if we love foolishness, we will do foolish, wrong, bad things.

Sometimes the call of foolishness comes from other people—from friends or even people we don't know who want us to do something wrong. The call of foolishness can come from a friend who tells you to lie to your mother or to be mean to another child.

Sometimes the call of foolishness comes from our own heart pulling us toward things that are wrong—like taking something that doesn't belong to us, choosing to disobey our parents, or watching television when we are supposed to be doing homework. Our own sinful hearts call us to love what is wrong.

What should we do when foolishness calls? If you said run away from it, you are right!

Do not enter the path of
the wicked,
 and do not walk in
the way of the evil.
Avoid it; do not go on it;
turn away from it and
pass on. (Proverbs 4:14–15)

We should turn away immediately from anything that is wrong or bad like lying, stealing, being mean to another person, or blaming someone else for something we did. It is very easy for our hearts to want to follow the call of foolishness. If you find your heart wanting something wrong or bad, ask God to give you a right heart.

You can't follow the call of wisdom and the call of foolishness at the same time, because they are two different paths, just like you can't sit down and stand up at the same time. You have to make a choice about which call to follow, which path to take—the way of wisdom or the way of foolishness.

We make these kinds of choices all the time. If you want to be a kind person, what sorts of things should you do? You should help others when things are hard for them, listen when they are upset, and give them a hug when they are sad. If you love kindness, you will do these things.

What kinds of things will you *not* do if you want to be kind? You will not hit people or call them names. You will not laugh at them when they make a mistake or grab the seat they want in class. You will run away from meanness because you love kindness. This is running away from the call of foolishness.

Suppose everyone in your class races to the water fountain after recess and you get there just before another boy. He becomes angry and says you pushed him out of the way—but you didn't. Maybe he even calls you a name. How can you run from the call of foolishness? Instead of calling him a name or pushing him, you could speak politely. You could remember the way of wisdom—"A soft answer turns away wrath" (Proverbs 15:1)—and follow it.

To walk on the path of wisdom and run from foolishness, you must read the Bible and hear the call of wisdom, but you must also pay attention to your heart. What does your heart want? Are you doing things that are good for your heart—to help your heart love the way of wisdom? You must guard your heart carefully.

> My son, be attentive to my words;
>   incline your ear to my sayings.
> Let them not escape from your sight;
>   keep them within your heart.
> For they are life to those who find them,
>   and healing to all their flesh.

> Keep your heart with all vigilance,
>   for from it flow the springs of life. (Proverbs 4:20–23)

To "keep your heart" means to watch over it, guard it, protect it. Ask yourself, "What does my heart want? Is that the way of wisdom—is it good and right?" To protect it from the way of foolishness means that you turn away from things that are not good for your heart—like friends who love foolishness. It means filling your heart with God's Word. Are you guarding your heart today? What are you doing to guard it?

> Keep hold of instruction; do not let go;
>   guard her, for she is your life. (Proverbs 4:13)

LEARNING TO TRUST GOD

- ✢ Does a person who is following the way of the wise ever do anything foolish? What is the difference between following the path of foolishness and doing something foolish? Read Proverbs 4:20–23 again. What can you do to guard your heart carefully?[1]

- ✢ Read Proverbs 2. What does it tell you about getting wisdom, the treasure of wisdom, and guarding your heart?

- ✢ *Activity:* Read and discuss Proverbs 4:26–27. Talk through some situations and note the foolish response and the wise response. Practice walking on a balance beam, a line on the floor, or the edge of a curb and consider how you can "ponder the path of your feet."

---

1. Make sure your child understands that even godly people who love God and want to walk in His ways sometimes sin. You want to help your child to see what *characterizes* his life—does his heart generally draw him toward wisdom or toward foolishness?

The Mocking Fool

What are some different kinds of shoes? There are sneakers for play, dress shoes for church, sandals, high heels, flip flops, baby booties. Though these are all different, they all have one thing the same: they are all shoes. Just as there are different kinds of shoes, there are different kinds of foolish people or "fools."[1] They are not all the same kind, but they are the same in one way. None of them walk in the way of the wise or love God and what is good and right. They do not obey God and do what is right.

One kind of fool is the "mocker" or "scoffer." A mocker is someone who makes fun of things. When the Bible talks about the mocker, it is talking about the person who makes fun of God, the things of God, and the people of God. This person is proud and does not respect God or see God as great. He makes fun of what is good and right. Can you think of any mockers in the Bible?

Pharaoh was a mocking fool. He was the king of Egypt, and he made the Hebrews be slaves. God sent Moses and Aaron to Pharaoh with the message to let the Hebrews go. Pharaoh's answer to God's message was the answer of a mocking fool.

> Who is the LORD, that I should obey his voice and let Israel go? I do not know the LORD, and moreover, I will not let Israel go. (Exodus 5:2)

What was wrong with Pharaoh's answer? Pharaoh did not honor or obey God. He did not fear God or see God's greatness. He thought he did not have to listen

---

1. Marvin Wilson, in his book *Our Father Abraham*, identifies various Hebrew words translated into English as our one word "fool." One such word is the Hebrew word *letz*. "This word means 'scoffer' or 'scorner.' . . . Proud, sneering, disrupting, and deriding, the *letz* is a master of heckling. He ridicules and pokes fun at all that is good and holy. He is . . . a troublemaker. He ignites controversy (Prov. 29:8), insults others (22:10), and acts haughtily (21:24). He knows all the answers; he turns his back to wisdom; he hates correction (Prov. 9:7–8)" (Marvin R. Wilson, *Our Father Abraham* [Grand Rapids: William B. Eerdmans, 1989], 286).

to God. He was a proud king of Egypt who mocked the great King of the whole world—God, the King of Kings.

The Roman soldiers who guarded Jesus after He was arrested were mocking fools, too. They did not treat Jesus as the Son of God. Instead, they beat Him.

> They also blindfolded him and kept asking him, "Prophesy! Who is it that struck you?" (Luke 22:64)

What terrible mocking hearts they had! They made fun of Jesus, doubting that He knew who hit Him—instead of bowing down to Him as the Son of God who knew every word they would ever say and everything they would ever do, who knows everything in the whole world.

When Jesus was crucified, two thieves were crucified with Him. One thief was a mocking fool. He would soon die and face God. He should have been horrified to face God with his sinful heart. He should have been begging Jesus for mercy. Instead, he mocked Jesus, saying,

Are you not the Christ? Save yourself and us! (Luke 23:39)

He wasn't asking Jesus for help. He was a mocking fool who did not believe that Jesus is the Savior of the world.

But the other thief was different. He said to the first thief,

Do you not fear God, since you are under the same sentence of condemnation? (Luke 23:40)

This thief knew that he was sinful, and he trembled at facing God. But the mocking thief had no fear of God. Mocking fools do not dread God's punishment of wrong or respect a holy and great God. They do not understand that they deserve God's terrible punishment.

A mocking fool may mock God for a while, but unless he trusts Jesus to forgive his sin and change his heart, his mocking will end in his destruction. He cannot mock God forever. He will not get away with being disrespectful to the God of all the earth.

Maybe you know some mocking fools—people who make fun of doing the right thing and don't respect what is good, people who don't care about the consequences of doing wrong and don't honor God, people who are cruel and proud and don't see the greatness of God. What kinds of things do these mockers do?

Perhaps someone might tell you about a movie he just got and invite you to watch it. It is not a nice movie and to watch it is not guarding your heart. If you are trusting in Jesus and walking in the way of the wise, what should you do? You should run away from foolishness! You should run away, even if the mocking fool mocks you.

What kind of mocking things might he say to you? He might make fun of you and call you a baby. He might say, "Are you afraid? What a scaredy-cat!" But it doesn't matter because you are following the path of wisdom. You are "keeping your heart with all vigilance." You are obeying God's Word in Psalm 1:

> Blessed is the man
> > who walks not in the counsel of the wicked,
> nor stands in the way of sinners,
> > nor sits in the seat of scoffers. (Psalm 1:1)

Blessed—happy—is the person who does not join in with mockers or scoffers, who does not act like them or do what they do. So don't copy their attitudes or try to be like them. They are mocking fools whose end is destruction unless they are rescued by Jesus.

> Do not swerve to the right or to the left;
> > turn your foot away from evil. (Proverbs 4:27)

LEARNING TO TRUST GOD

✣ Read Psalm 1:1–2. What does it mean to not walk in the counsel of the wicked, or stand in the way of sinners, or sit in the seat of scoffers? What does verse 2 tell you about the way of the wise?

✣ Read Proverbs 3. What does it say about the person who finds wisdom? Why is this person blessed?

✣ *Activity:* How can you meditate on God's Word day and night? As a family, choose a verse to meditate on, and then think of one way to help you meditate on that verse. At the end of the week, share what God has shown you through meditating on that verse.

The Rebellious Fool

Have you ever heard the names Hophni and Phinehas? They are odd names, but they are the real names of the two sons of the priest Eli, and they were priests, too. But they were not good priests. They were rebellious, insisting on their own way instead of obeying God's way.[1]

People made offerings to God as a way to ask forgiveness for their sins. The offerings were made by the priests in certain respectful ways. But Hophni and Phinehas were not respectful of the offerings, and they decided to do things their own way. Instead of poking their forks into the offering pots of boiled meat and eating the meat that came up on the fork, they took their meat before it went into the pot. This way they could take a bigger piece and the best meat for themselves. They did not respect God or care about the offerings.

Hophni and Phinehas also did other evil things. Their father, Eli, heard about the evil things they were doing. So Eli warned his sons about their evil behavior and their disrespect for God and His law. But Hophni and Phinehas did not listen to him. They were stubborn, rebellious fools.[2]

Do you know what a rebellious fool is? A rebellious fool is stubborn and does not listen to good advice. He insists on doing things his own wrong way. He does not learn from his mistakes. When he is warned about his evil, foolish ways, he keeps on doing wrong and bad things instead of repenting—turning away from his sin.

---

1. See 1 Samuel 2:12–17, 22–26, for their story.
2. Another fool is portrayed by the Hebrew words *kesil* and *ewil*. "They often refer to a person who is 'thick-headed,' 'dull-witted,' or 'dense' in the sense of moral deficiency. The idea of thickness suggests a hardened, sluggish and obstinate person, slow to change his ways. . . . The *kesil* is so self-confident that he is set in his ways. He is also strong-willed, refusing to learn readily. Hence, his propensity is to disregard moral ideals. He persists in evil. . . . The *ewil* shares many of the same marks of senselessness and moral impropriety. This fool rejects instruction (Prov. 12:15), babbles thoughtlessly (10:14), and is quick-tempered (14:29). Furthermore, the *ewil* quarrels (20:3) and rages (29:9). Coarse and hardened, he will not be broken (27:22). In his insolence, he mocks at sin (14:9)" (Marvin R. Wilson, *Our Father Abraham* [Grand Rapids: Eerdmans, 1989], 285–86).

And this is just what Hophni and Phinehas did. They would not listen to their father's good warning or turn from their wrong ways. Their stubborn, rebellious hearts kept them following the way of the foolish.

Do you know what happened to these two sons of Eli? The prophet Samuel told Eli that his sons would both die on the same day. And guess what happened? Just as the prophet said, the two sons of Eli, Hophni and Phinehas, both died on the same day in a battle against the Philistines. They were destroyed because of their evil, stubborn, rebellious hearts.

Proverbs has some words of advice to help us run from the foolishness of Hophni and Phinehas:

> My son, do not forget my teaching,
>   but let your heart keep my commandments,
>   for length of days and years of life
>   and peace they will add to you. (Proverbs 3:1–2)

What does this verse tell you *not* to do? It tells you not to forget the good teaching of your parents. What does it tell you to do instead? To keep your parents' rules and God's good law.

But wisdom must be in our hearts, not just in our

heads. It is not enough to *know* these verses. We must *do* them. Hophni and Phinehas heard their father's words, but they did not keep his commands. They *knew* the commands, but they didn't *do* them . . . and they died because of their foolishness.

The Bible tells us about another son who was a stubborn, rebellious fool. Do you know who he was? He was the son of a king.

It was Absalom, the son of King David. Absalom did not honor or listen to the wise teaching of his father. He did not love wisdom in his heart. He killed his brother, and he tried to take his father's throne—he tried to be king. He gathered together men to join him in rebelling against his father.

Do you know what happened to this rebellious fool? In a battle against his father's men, Absalom got his long, thick hair caught in a tree, and a soldier named Joab stabbed him through the heart with three spears. Absalom died a rebellious fool.[3]

David grieved for his son Absalom. Even though Absalom was a rebellious fool, David loved him, and grieved over his son's foolishness.

> To have a fool for a son brings grief;
>   there is no joy for the father of a fool. (Proverbs 17:21, NIV)

These are very sad stories of sons who were rebellious fools; sons who brought great sorrow to their fathers and were destroyed.

The Bible also has a very happy story in it. It is the story of a Son who did not bring sorrow to his Father; a Son who listened to and obeyed the commands of his Father; a Son who loved wisdom and what is right; a Son who did not insist on his own way but did what is right even when it was hard. Do you know who that Son was? He was Jesus, the perfect Son of God who brought pure joy to His Father as an obedient Son. This is what God said about Jesus:

---

3. See 2 Samuel 15–18.

This is my beloved Son, with whom I am well pleased. (Matthew 3:17)

Jesus brought much joy to his Father because He was wise. He loved what is right and obeyed His Father.

> *A wise son makes a glad father,*
> *but a foolish son is a sorrow to his mother (Proverbs 10:1).*

What kind of son or daughter do you want to be?

LEARNING TO TRUST GOD

✣ Read the story of Hophni and Phinehas in 2 Samuel 2:12–36. In what ways were they rebellious fools? What was the consequence of their foolishness?

✣ Read Proverbs 4. What good advice is in this chapter? How can you follow it?

✣ *Activity:* Talk as a family about the teachings or instructions of your parents. Make a booklet of this wise counsel. Then share the booklet with someone else.

The Godless Fool

What do you do with the wrapper when you unwrap a candy bar? You throw it away. You don't want or need it.

That is the way some people treat God. They don't want God, and they don't think they need Him. They are godless fools.[1]

> The fool says in his heart, "There is no God."
>   They are corrupt, they do abominable deeds,
>   there is none who does good. (Psalm 14:1)

Not all godless fools would say with their words that there is no God. Some of them might *say* there is a God, but they *live* like there is no God. They fill their lives with so many other things that they have no room for God. They never think about God or what He wants. They never read the Bible. They don't talk about God, pray about decisions, or look in the Bible for advice. They are without God; they are godless.

Walking in wisdom or foolishness is a "heart thing." It is not just about what you know or say. It is about what you have in your heart. The fool says in his *heart* that there is no God. He may say with his mouth that there is a God, but in his heart he has no room for God. He doesn't love, think about, or care about God. The things that are important to God do not matter to him at all.

---

1. A third Hebrew word for fool is *nabal*. "Perhaps the most pointed meaning of this word is found in Psalm 14:1: 'The fool [*nabal*] says in his heart, "There is no God."' Such distorted thinking by this fool typifies that of the 'wicked,' of whom the psalmist says, 'in all his thoughts there is no room for God' (Ps. 10:4). Devoid of spiritual perception, the *nabal* has a closed mind—at the moment—to the 'God-idea.' Thus the *nabal* is arrogant (Prov. 17:7). . . . Isaiah indicates that this impiety of the *nabal* also includes moral depravity (he is 'busy with evil') and social insensitivity ('the hungry he leaves empty and from the thirsty he withholds water'–32:6). . . . Through 'vile deeds' (Ps. 14:1) the fool states, as it were, that the living reality of God is missing from human experience" (Marvin R. Wilson, *Our Father Abraham* [Grand Rapids: Eerdmans, 1989], 286–87).

Jesus told a story about a godless fool. We don't know his name. The Bible just calls him "the rich man." He had fine clothes, good food, and a nice house. Outside the gates of the rich man's house there was a poor man named Lazarus. Lazarus was covered with sores and was very hungry. He was so hungry that he wanted the leftover food from the rich man's meals. But the rich man did not care about Lazarus. He wouldn't even share the food that fell from his table.

The poor man died and went to heaven. The Bible says that he "was carried by the angels to Abraham's side" (Luke 6:22). Isn't that a beautiful thought?

The rich man died, too . . . but what happened to him wasn't beautiful at all. He was buried, and no angels carried him to heaven. Instead, he was in torment in the fires of hell—in excruciating pain and suffering. He was so awfully thirsty that he called to Abraham and asked him to send Lazarus to touch his tongue with wet fingers. The man who wouldn't give Lazarus a scrap of food, was now asking for water from Lazarus!

What do you think Abraham said? He told him that there was a great, wide gorge or valley between heaven and hell, and it is impossible to cross it. The rich man was forever in hell, and there was no help for him.

But maybe there was hope for his family on earth. The rich man thought that if someone like Lazarus came from the dead to warn his brothers about the horrors of hell, they would turn from their foolish ways and turn to God. But Abraham knew better. The rich man's brothers already had the teaching of Moses and the prophets. They knew about God . . . but they, too, were godless fools, with no room in their hearts for God.

What do you think Abraham told the rich man? He said to the rich man,

> If they do not hear Moses and the Prophets, neither will they be convinced if someone should rise from the dead. (Luke 16:31)

It isn't that the godless fool doesn't know about God. The problem is that he doesn't desire God. He loves other things more than he loves God. There is no room in his thoughts or his heart for God because he has filled his heart with other things.

Do you know what that is like? It is like packing your backpack for school. If you cram it full of shoes and books, a jacket and hat, markers and crayons, and maybe a few treasures from your room—like your favorite toys—you won't have any room for your lunch!

We can do the same thing with our hearts. We can fill them with so many other things—sports and games, friends and fun, toys and money—that we have no room for God. We have no time for or desire for God in our lives. We can seek after so many things in this world that God is not important to us at all.

But did you know that every single person has been created by God with a desire for God that cannot be filled by anything else—even when that person tries to push God out of his life and doesn't make any room for God?

What is important to you? Do you want to be a godless fool who thinks he does not need God? Or do you want to seek God and seek wisdom . . . and live forever in heaven like Lazarus?

**In the pride of his face the wicked does not seek him;
all his thoughts are, "There is no God." (Psalm 10:4)**

LEARNING TO TRUST GOD

✦ Read Philippians 3:7–9. How was Paul different from the rich man? What are you filling your life with? What do you treasure most?

✦ Read Proverbs 6. What can you learn about wisdom and foolishness from this chapter?

✦ *Activity:* Do you have room for God in your life? As a family, look at your calendar. What does it tell you about what is important to you? Do you need to make changes? How will you make these changes? Make a calendar for the month that intentionally makes room for God.

The Simple Fool

Would it be easier to convince your father that a man from outer space visited you last night, or to make a small child believe it? Why? A little child doesn't have the understanding of an adult. There is so much little children do not know. Most young children believe whatever you tell them. But as they grow older, they learn that they can't believe and follow everything they are told.

There are some people who are like a small child, people who easily believe what others say because they don't think for themselves. The Bible calls them simple fools.[1] The simple fool is like a person who hasn't grown up. He often believes whatever he hears and doesn't stop to think about whether it is right or true. But wise people are not like that.

> The simple believes everything,
> > but the prudent gives thought to his steps. (Proverbs 14:15)

The prudent or wise man thinks about what he is doing—he gives thought to his steps. He thinks about what he has heard and decides whether it is true. He asks God to help him to be wise and to know what is right and wrong. He thinks about what will happen if he follows what he has heard. In his heart, he wants to do what is right and good.

---

[1]. A fourth Hebrew word for fool is *peti* or *pethi*. It is "often translated 'simple.' The word derives from a root suggesting the idea of being 'open, spacious, wide.' *Peti* is the term for 'fool' which carries with it the greatest potential that one will welcome instruction and correction from a wise man. One who is 'open' is accessible. Though often immature, inexperienced, and easily led into all kinds of enticement, the *peti* is, fortunately, teachable. A 'simple' one might be naïve, gullible, and easily fooled (see Prov. 7:7ff.), yet his mind is not barred to the entrance of wisdom. Openness has the potential of being turned into virtue as quickly as vice. . . . The *peti* is a person who is usually approachable and hence educable. . . . His folly could be corrected" (Marvin R. Wilson, *Our Father Abraham* [Grand Rapids: William B. Eerdmans, 1989], 284–85).

But the simple fool is eager to believe anything. He doesn't stop to think or check out if something is right. He doesn't think about what might happen if he follows the ideas of others; he just follows them. The simple fool does not have a brain problem . . . he has a heart problem. Doing what is right and good is not important to him.

You can be the kind of person who just takes the suggestions of others without thinking about whether they are good or bad . . . and find yourself in all kinds of foolish trouble. Or you can be prudent or wise and give thought to your steps, like David in the Bible.

King Saul wanted to kill David because he was very jealous of David. So David and his men hid from Saul in the wilderness. When Saul heard that David was in the wilderness, he went looking for David. Saul went into a cave, but stayed near the opening. What he didn't know was that David and his men were hiding further inside the cave!

What idea do you think David's men had? Saul didn't know they were in the cave, so David's men suggested that David sneak up and kill Saul! That way, Saul couldn't kill David.

What do you think a simple fool would do about this? A simple fool would probably follow the suggestion of the men. He would not stop to think about whether it was right or wrong, or what God would want him to do. He would just do it.

But David wasn't a simple fool. He loved God and wanted to walk in the way of the wise. He sneaked up to Saul . . . but he didn't kill him. He only cut off part of Saul's robe. He did not listen to the bad advice of his men.

But then David felt bad about cutting the robe and said to his men,

> The LORD forbid that I should do this thing to my lord, the LORD's anointed, to put out my hand against him, seeing he is the LORD's anointed. (1 Samuel 24:6)

David didn't do what his men suggested. He gave "thought to his steps." He knew it was wrong to hurt the man God had made to be king of Israel, so he did the right thing. He didn't kill Saul, but let him live.

Would you like to be like David, giving thought to your steps and following the way of the wise? It is easy to be a simple fool, not thinking for yourself and just following what others tell you. It is especially easy for children to follow the way of foolishness because sometimes you don't even know what is right or wrong.

That is why it is important to read God's Word and learn about what is right. Listening to the good teaching of your parents can make you wise, too. So can choosing wise and godly friends. Do you know why it is so important to choose good friends? Because people are like celery. Celery? Yes, celery.

This is how people are like celery. If you put celery in colored water, the celery drinks up the colored water. Do you know what happens to the celery? It becomes the color of the water! So if you put celery in red water, after a while you will have red celery!

People are like celery because very often they become like the people they are with. They "drink up" the ideas, desires, habits, and behavior of those around them. So if you want to be wise, you must be around wise people, not foolish people.

> Whoever walks with the wise becomes wise,
>   but the companion of fools will suffer harm. (Proverbs 13:20)

LEARNING TO TRUST GOD

✣ Read the story of David and Saul in 1 Samuel 24. How was David different from Saul? Do you think and pray about what others tell you, or do you just follow them? Give an example from your life.

✣ Read Proverbs 8. What does this chapter tell you to listen to?

✣ *Activity:* As a family, try the celery-in-water experiment using a leafy stalk. Then talk about the kinds of "influences" around you. Will they lead you into what is wise or what is foolish? Do you need to make any changes?

Foolishness Leads to Destruction

Have you ever watched the water in a sink or bathtub after the drain is opened? What happens to it? It goes around and around and around . . . and then it gets sucked down, down, down into the drain.

This is what the path of foolishness is like. Wisdom calls aloud, but if wisdom is ignored there are bad consequences—and a person gets sucked down into the drain of destruction.

> How long, O simple ones, will you love being simple?
> How long will scoffers delight in their scoffing
>   and fools hate knowledge?
> . . . .
> Because I have called and you refused to listen,
>   have stretched out my hand and no one has heeded,
> because you have ignored all my counsel
>   and would have none of my reproof,
> I also will laugh at your calamity;
>   I will mock when terror strikes you,
> . . . .
> For the simple are killed by their turning away,
>   and the complacency of fools destroys them. (Proverbs 1:22, 24–26, 32)

The Bible tells us about a man who did not listen to the call of wisdom . . . not just one time but many times. The man was King Saul, the first king of Israel. He did not give thought to his steps or run from foolishness. Instead, he loved what is wrong and bad. He did not repent or turn away from his foolishness, but continued down the path of foolishness to destruction.

When Israel was going into battle with the Philistines, Saul did not wait for Samuel, the priest, to come and offer a sacrifice to God. Instead, he disobeyed God's command that only the priests were to offer sacrifices and he did it himself. He was a simple fool who did not give thought to his steps. He rebelled against God's ways, doing things his own way instead.

And Samuel said to Saul, "You have done foolishly. You have not kept the command of the Lord your God, with which he commanded you. For then the Lord would have established your kingdom over Israel forever. But now your kingdom shall not continue. The Lord has sought out a man after his own heart, and the Lord has commanded him to be prince over his people, because you have not kept what the Lord commanded you." (1 Samuel 13:13–14)

What a terrible consequence for Saul's stubborn foolishness. He lost the royal line of kingship—God would choose another king. But Saul did not repent and turn from foolishness.

In order to punish the evil Amalekites, God told Saul to attack the Amalekites and destroy everything—even the animals. Saul fought the Amalekites, but he did not kill Agag, the Amalekite king. And he kept the best of the sheep, cattle, calves, and lambs. He listened to people who wanted to keep the animals. Was this obeying the Lord? Was it following the way of the wise? Saul was a rebellious fool who insisted on doing things his way and not God's way. He was a simple fool listening to the bad advice of the people instead of listening to God. Then Saul lied and told Samuel that he had destroyed everything.

Just like water in a drain, Saul went down, down, down to destruction. Instead of turning from foolishness, Saul became jealous of David and tried to kill him. His sin sucked him down into more sin and he killed 85 priests just because one priest helped David.

But Saul still did not turn away from loving and doing what is wrong and bad. He continued down the path of foolishness. This time, Saul was a mocking fool.

Israel was at war with the Philistines and Saul wondered what would happen in the battle, so he asked God if Israel would win. But God did not answer Saul. Because Saul refused to turn away from his foolish sin, God turned away from Saul.

What do you think Saul did when God would not answer him? He went to a witch for the answer to his question! Saul foolishly turned from God to someone who mocked God. Saul ignored the path of wisdom. He was being sucked into the drain of destruction.

Finally, Saul did one last foolish act. In a battle with the Philistines, Saul was wounded. But he did not want to be killed by the Philistines, so Saul took his own sword, fell on it, and killed himself. What a foolish path of destruction Saul took. What a sad end he had following the way of foolishness!

Foolishness is loving and doing what is wrong and bad. Over and over, Saul turned away from wisdom. He refused to run from sin and ask for God's help. Saul knew what was right . . . but he didn't do it. He chose what is wrong, even though he knew it was wrong, because he did not love what is right and good.

Foolishness brings destruction—here on earth and then forever in hell. Wisdom brings life and joy here and then forever in heaven. Wisdom and foolishness are calling out to you. Which path will you take?

> For the simple are killed by their turning away,
>   and the complacency of fools destroys them;
> but whoever listens to me will dwell secure
>   and will be at ease, without dread of disaster. (Proverbs 1:32–33)

LEARNING TO TRUST GOD

✤ Read 1 Samuel 15. Where do you see the foolishness of Saul? Saul said he had sinned, but did he truly repent?[1]

✤ Read Proverbs 9. What do verses 9 and 10 show as the difference between the foolish man and the wise man? Why is the fear of the Lord the beginning of wisdom?

✤ *Activity:* Mom or Dad, share your testimony with your family, noting how God turned you from the path of foolishness, or ask someone else to share his testimony with your family. What can you do to graciously warn someone of the destruction of foolishness and the joy of wisdom? Act on one of your ideas this week.

---

1. Make sure your child understands the difference between being sorry about the consequences of sin, and turning from sin in true repentance because you hate your sin and the offense it is to God.

Driving Out Folly

Have you ever tried to peel off a price tag from something? Is it easy? Sometimes the sticker is stuck on really hard and you can only remove it in pieces . . . and getting off all the glue is even harder. Knowing about how hard it is to get the stickers off can help us to understand our hearts.

Our hearts are like something with a sticker on it. We have something stuck in our hearts that is really hard to get off. We are born with foolishness in our hearts. Foolishness is a love for the wrong things. Being selfish and unkind, or angry and pouty, is really easy for us. We are born loving ourselves more than we love God and His ways—and this is really stuck on our hearts.

Look into your own heart. Do you find the foolishness of rebellion and insisting on doing things your own way? How about the unwillingness to obey what is right? Or the foolishness of ignoring God and making other things more important than God? Is that in your heart? Does your heart want to follow the crowd, listening to the suggestions of others instead of asking if it is God's way? These things are in all of our hearts. We are born with foolish hearts loving the wrong things.

> Folly is bound up in the heart of a child,
>   but the rod of discipline drives it far from him. (Proverbs 22:15)

"Folly" is another word for foolishness. The Bible says that it is in your heart. We do not need to learn to love what is wrong—that is easy for us. If your mother gave you a piece of your favorite candy and said you could eat it or give it to your brother or sister, would it be easier to keep it for yourself or to give it away? The folly of selfishness is in our hearts naturally; generosity is not. We need to *learn* to love what is right. That is hard to do, and only Jesus can do this for us.

God is so good that He has given us a special tool to help "unstick" the folly or foolishness that is in our hearts. Do you know what this tool is? Listen to this verse again:

> Folly is bound up in the heart of a child,
> but the rod of discipline drives it far from him. (Proverbs 22:15)

What is the special tool? Yes, it is discipline—consequences, reprimands, spankings, time-outs; discipline drives out folly. God, in His great goodness, has given children parents to discipline them because He knows how dangerous foolishness is. This discipline drives out the folly in your hearts. What a good God we have!

Can you think of a time in the Bible when God disciplined His children? One time was when Miriam and Aaron were speaking wrongly against Moses. They were jealous of Moses because God spoke to Moses in a special way as the leader of His people. Instead of trusting God's wisdom, they were angry that God had chosen Moses as the leader. Their hearts were very foolish, full of rebellion and jealousy.

Did God ignore the sinful behavior of Miriam and Aaron? To do that would be to let foolishness grow in their hearts. God would not do that. He is a loving Father to His children. So God defended Moses, and then He disciplined Miriam and Aaron:

> When the cloud removed from over the tent, behold, Miriam was leprous, like snow. And Aaron turned toward Miriam, and behold, she was leprous. (Numbers 12:10)

What did God do? He gave Miriam a terrible disease called leprosy. Leprosy ate away at a person's body, and there was no cure for it. It was a terrible punishment.

Do you know why God gave such a terrible punishment? Because He is good and loving. He knew Miriam and Aaron needed to have the folly driven out of their hearts. This bad consequence helped Aaron and Miriam see how serious their sin was:

> And Aaron said to Moses, "Oh, my lord, do not punish us because we have done foolishly and have sinned." (Numbers 12:11)

Aaron and Miriam repented—they turned away from their foolishness. They said "No" to the way of foolishness and set their feet on the path of wisdom. Foolishness does not have to lead to destruction. If you let discipline turn your heart to repentance and back to the way of wisdom, foolishness can be driven out—or unstuck—from your heart.

When Aaron and Miriam repented and turned from the sin in their hearts, God healed Miriam. He allowed the punishment to do its job, and then with great kindness God took away the punishment. Isn't He a good God?

Do you see discipline as a good thing? Do you believe it is a gift from God and from your parents? Let's thank God for discipline that drives folly out of our hearts and ask Him to give us hearts that love what is good and right.

My son, do not despise the L<small>ORD</small>'s discipline
> or be weary of his reproof,
for the L<small>ORD</small> reproves him whom he loves,
> as a father the son in whom he delights. (Proverbs 3:11–12)

LEARNING TO TRUST GOD

✢ Read Numbers 12 and Hebrews 12:5–11. How does the discipline of Miriam and Aaron show the truth of Hebrews 12:5–11? Pray that you will respond rightly to discipline.

✢ Read Proverbs 10. Are there any verses in this chapter that can encourage you to drive folly out of your heart?

✢ *Activity:* Mom or Dad, tell your family about a time when you were disciplined and the good result of that discipline. As a family, make a special treat to bless another family. Ask God to give you a generous heart and to drive out the folly of selfishness.

Get Wisdom

Which is easier to erase—a mark from a pencil or a mark from a pen? Of course, a pencil mark is easier.

Driving folly out of the heart of a person who wants wisdom is more like erasing a pencil mark than a pen mark. But driving folly out of the heart of a person who isn't seeking wisdom and is content to walk in foolishness is more like erasing a pen mark. It is very hard because the unwise person does not learn from discipline or instruction.

The hard heart is the heart that loves foolishness. Only God can change a hard heart into a wise heart. We all have foolish hearts that love what is wrong and bad. But when a person trusts in Jesus to forgive his sins and be his Savior, Jesus gives that person a new heart—a heart that wants to walk in the way of the wise.

Then that person loves wisdom and wants more and more to learn what is good and right and how to walk in God's ways. He knows wisdom is a treasure that protects us from what is wrong and hurtful. When he is disciplined, he is glad when the folly is driven out of his heart. He wants to please God and do what is right, so he looks for wisdom.

> Get wisdom; get insight;
> 	do not forget, and do not turn away from the words of my mouth.
> Do not forsake her, and she will keep you;
> 	love her, and she will guard you. (Proverbs 4:5–6)

But where does he look for wisdom? How does he get it?

> The fear of the Lord is the beginning of wisdom,
> 	and the knowledge of the Holy One is insight. (Proverbs 9:10)

He finds wisdom by learning to fear the Lord. Does this mean that you should be afraid of God? Maybe a story from Exodus will help you to understand about the fear of the Lord.

When Moses and the people of Israel were camped at Mount Sinai, Moses told them that the Lord would come down on the mountain to speak to them. He warned them that if anyone even touched the mountain, he would be put to death.

On the third day, there was a thick cloud on the mountain. There was thunder, lightning, and a very loud trumpet blast, which grew louder and louder. Smoke went up from the mountain and the whole mountain trembled! The people were so afraid that they were trembling, too! Would you have trembled?

They were so afraid of the power of God that they said to Moses,

You speak to us, and we will listen; but do not let God speak to us, lest we die. (Exodus 20:19)

Would you say they were afraid of God? Yes, they were very afraid! But Moses said to them:

Do not be afraid. God has come to test you, so that the fear of God will be with you to keep you from sinning. (Exodus 20:20, NIV)

Moses told them not to be afraid . . . but to fear God. Doesn't that sound strange? What does it mean?

Would you be afraid of a mean boy who beat up other kids, punching them in the stomach and pulling their hair? Why might you be afraid? You would be afraid because you don't trust him and think he might hurt you, too.

But do you feel the same way about your father? Your father is stronger than the mean boy, but you probably aren't afraid of him. You don't tremble when he walks into the room. You know he loves you, and even though he is strong, he is also good.

You aren't afraid of your strong dad, but you do fear him. If he tells you to clean your room and you play outside instead, and he finds out, you feel fear. But you trust your father. You know he still loves you even though you disappointed him. There is a fear of displeasing your father and of the consequences of disobeying him.

Just like the fear of your father is different from being afraid of him, so the fear of the Lord is different from being afraid of Him. God is strong and powerful. The Bible calls Him "a consuming fire" (Deuteronomy 4:24). God can destroy anything and everything. He punishes evil and sent fire from heaven to destroy Sodom and Gomorrah. When we sin, we should fear God's discipline and His holy hatred of sin.

But God is always good to His children. He is patient and understands their weakness. When He disciplines, He disciplines in love. So even though God is very powerful, He is also good. Fearing God is fearing what God could do, and it is also trusting Him to do what is right.

Do you know what dynamite is? It is a powerful explosive used to blow openings in mountains so roads and tunnels can be built through them. You should fear what dynamite can do. But dynamite is also a very good help in building roads. A person who knows how to use dynamite is not afraid of it, but he does fear or respect what it can do.

It is the same with God. If you know and love God as His child, you are not afraid of Him, but you do fear Him. You know He is powerful, but you also know that He is good and you can trust Him. Do you know and love God?

> The fear of the Lord is the beginning of wisdom,
>   and the knowledge of the Holy One is insight. (Proverbs 9:10)

LEARNING TO TRUST GOD

✣ Read Exodus 19–20:21. What should the people of Israel—and you—be afraid of? What shows you that God is good and loving? Explain the difference between being afraid of God and fearing Him. Who should be afraid of God?

✣ Read Proverbs 11. Choose a verse to memorize and share with someone this week.

✣ *Activity:* Read the conversation between the children and Mr. and Mrs. Beaver in *The Lion, the Witch and the Wardrobe* regarding the return of Aslan.[1] Or watch the Disney movie version of *The Chronicles of Narnia: The Lion, the Witch and the Wardrobe*. What did Mr. Beaver mean when he said that Aslan (representing God in the story) "isn't safe" but "good"?

1. See *The Lion, the Witch and the Wardrobe,* by C. S. Lewis, chapter 8.

Fearing God: Who He Is

Let's think about lights. A candle can give a glow to a small space. A flashlight gives a beam of light. A lightbulb can light up a whole room. But the sun lights up half the world at a time! Wow! No light compares to the sun. It is the greatest light in our solar system[1]—there is nothing like it. It is in a group all by itself, and nothing else is enough like the sun to be in that group. It is one of a kind.

God is in a group by Himself, too—a group that *nothing in the whole universe* is part of. He is so much greater than everything and everyone. He is so awesome, amazing, and magnificent that nothing compares to Him.

> To whom then will you compare me,
> that I should be like him? says the Holy One. (Isaiah 40:25)

God is in a group by Himself—only He belongs in it, because nothing can be compared to Him. When a person truly understands and feels the enormous greatness of God, he is starting to understand what it means to fear the Lord.

This happened to Simon Peter when he was fishing. Do you want to hear about it?

Simon Peter and his friends were fishermen. They had been fishing all night, but they didn't catch anything. So they brought their boats back to shore and began to wash their nets. A big crowd of people were there, trying to get to Jesus. So Jesus got into Simon Peter's boat to have some room to teach the people.

> And when he had finished speaking, he said to Simon, "Put out into the deep and let down your nets for a catch." (Luke 5:4)

---

[1]. You may need to simply explain the solar system as the sun and all the bodies that orbit or circle the sun—planets, asteroids, meteors, comets, satellites.

The fishermen were tired and had just cleaned their nets, and now Jesus wanted them to go fishing! This was not the time to catch fish!

And Simon answered, "Master, we toiled all night and took nothing! But at your word I will let down the nets." (Luke 5:5)

What do you think happened when the fishermen obeyed Jesus? They caught a lot of fish! The net was *filled* with fish—all kinds of fish. So many fish that the nets began to break! They had to ask their partners in another boat to help them. They filled both boats so full of fish that they began to sink! How many fish do you think were in those nets?

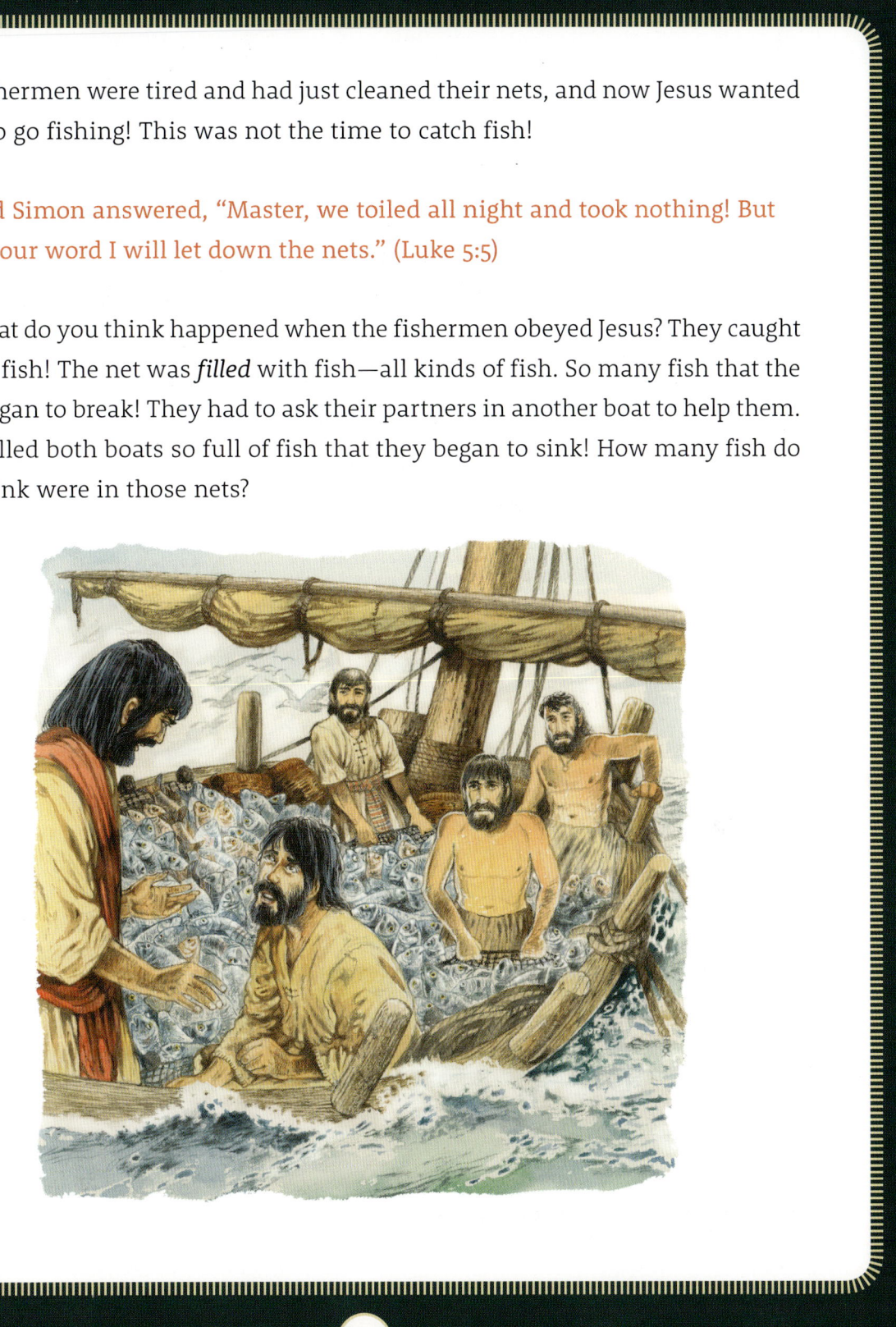

When Simon Peter saw the fish miracle, he understood that Jesus is God. He saw the greatness of Jesus. He truly understood and felt that Jesus was greater than anything or anyone. So he fell to his knees and worshipped Jesus.

When Simon Peter saw the greatness of Jesus—when he saw how magnificent and awesome Jesus is—he realized that he could not compare at all to Jesus. He saw how much greater Jesus was than he was.

> He fell down at Jesus' knees, saying, "Depart from me, for I am a sinful man, O Lord." (Luke 5:8)

Why did Simon Peter ask Jesus to leave him? Why did he call Jesus "Lord"? Why did he realize that he was such a sinful man?

Simon Peter wasn't worshipping Jesus because he was excited about all the fish. He worshipped Jesus because he saw who Jesus is—the Son of God, the one to whom no one can be compared, the one who is so great that He is in a group all by Himself. The fish miracle helped him to see the greatness of Jesus. What Simon Peter felt in his heart was awe, wonder, amazement at who Jesus is—at the greatness of Jesus. He saw that Jesus is God.

When he saw who Jesus is, deep in his heart and soul Peter understood that he was not worthy to be near Jesus. He was nothing compared to Jesus. He was a sinful man who had no right to be in a boat with the Son of God. In his heart was a fear of the Lord—a respect for who Jesus is, an understanding of His one-of-a-kind greatness.

Do you want to know the most amazing part of this story? This great, one-of-a-kind, in-a-group-all-His-own Jesus did not want to leave Simon Peter. He called Simon Peter to be His disciple—His follower—to tell others about the greatness of God. He wanted Simon Peter to be His friend.

This same great, one-of-a-kind, in-a-group-all-His-own Jesus wants you to know Him and be His friend, too. Even though He is greater than any king or president, you can talk to Him at any time. You don't even need an appointment. He watches over the whole world, and He watches over you. Can you believe that such a God would love sinners like you and me? Have you seen His greatness and worth and worshipped Him like Peter did?

> For who in the skies can be compared to the Lord?
> Who among the heavenly beings is like the Lord,
> a God greatly to be feared in the council of the holy ones,
> and awesome above all who are around him? (Psalm 89:6–7)

LEARNING TO TRUST GOD

✢ Read Luke 5:1–11. Try to imagine how Simon Peter felt. What made him feel that way? Have you ever realized how unimportant you are compared to Jesus, or how sinful you are compared to a Holy God? If you can begin to feel this, you will begin to understand the fear of the Lord.

✢ Read Proverbs 12. Find one proverb that is important wisdom for you. Write it on a card and memorize it this week. At the end of the week, tell your family what you learned from this verse.

✢ *Activity:* We can't begin to understand the greatness of God and how unworthy we are. This week do one activity that will help you see that God is in a category all His own, something that shows you the greatness of God (e.g., go on a nature hike, look at the stars at night, ponder the animals at the zoo, examine snowflakes, list as many bugs as you can). How does this show you the greatness of God?

Fearing God: What He Is Like— Perfect in Everything

Have you ever watched the Olympic games? Some of the best athletes in the world show how good they are in their sports. They practice very hard to be good at their one sport. When the scorecards are shown, they want their marks to be the highest.

We admire—respect and appreciate—Olympic athletes because they are really good at their sports . . . but God is good at *everything*. What kind of score should God get for being good at everything? Nothing is hard for God. He doesn't have to practice at anything—He is just perfect in every way.

> Ah, Lord God! It is you who have made the heavens and the earth by your great power and by your outstretched arm! Nothing is too hard for you. (Jeremiah 32:17)

Do you remember how God made the world? He just spoke! That's power! His words alone are enough to create the heavens and the earth, the stars . . . the whole universe! Who else can create anything just by their words alone? No one compares to God.

> By the word of the Lord the heavens were made,
>   and by the breath of his mouth all their host.
> He gathers the waters of the sea as a heap;
>   he puts the deeps in storehouses.
>
> Let all the earth fear the Lord;
>   let all the inhabitants of the world stand in awe of him!

> For he spoke, and it came to be;
> he commanded, and it stood firm. (Psalm 33:6–9)

Do you stand in awe of God? God is not just "good at everything He does." He is more than good. He is *perfect* in everything He does and all that He is. He is perfect in power, perfect in knowledge, perfect in love, perfect in beauty, perfect in justice, perfect in mercy, perfect in truthfulness . . . perfect in everything.

No one knows what God knows.

> He determines the number of the stars;
>> he gives to all of them their names. (Psalm 147:4)

Can you imagine knowing the names of every single star? There are 100 billion stars in our galaxy, which is our part of the universe. That is a lot of stars! But our galaxy is only one galaxy. Scientists think that there might be 100 billion galaxies in the universe—and every one of them has billions of stars. We can't even imagine how many stars that is. But God knows the name of every single one of them! What does this tell you about what God is like?

If we admire an Olympic athlete, how much more should we be in awe of God? We should be in awe of God for who He is—because He is God. And we should admire God because of what He is like. This is the fear of the Lord—being in awe of God because He is God, and admiring God because of the kind of person He is.

To fear the Lord—to admire God because of what He is like—is also to trust Him. We know we can trust Him because He is perfect in power and perfect in love for His children.

Do you remember how God saved His people in Egypt? He showed them His awesome power by sending ten plagues to free them from the rule of the Egyptians. He turned water into blood; He sent frogs, gnats, flies, boils, hail, grasshopper-like locusts—thousands and thousands of them; He made darkness over all the land; and He sent death to their animals and their firstborn sons. None of these plagues was hard for God to do.

When Pharaoh finally let the Hebrews (Israel) go, he sent his armies after them. With the Red Sea in front of them and the armies behind them, the people of God had no place to go. They were stuck with a huge problem.

But it wasn't a problem for God. He just sent a big wind to open up a path across the sea for His people. That is amazing! But even more amazing is that when the Egyptians followed the sea path, God closed the water over them . . . and not one of the enemies of God's people lived.

Do you know what the people of Israel did when they saw the power of God at work to save them?

> And when the Israelites saw the great power the Lord displayed against the Egyptians, the people feared the Lord and put their trust in him and in Moses his servant. (Exodus 14:31 NIV)

The Israelites feared the Lord because they saw what He is like. They were in awe of God's power and His love for them. They could trust Him because He had used His power to rescue them. God loved them and worked for their good.

Are you in awe of God because of what He is like? If you are His child, you can trust Him to do good to you, too.

> There is none like you, O Lord;
>   you are great, and your name is great in might.
> Who would not fear you, O King of the nations?
>   For this is your due;
> for among all the wise ones of the nations
>   and in all their kingdoms
>   there is none like you. (Jeremiah 10:6–7)

LEARNING TO TRUST GOD

✢ Read Jeremiah 10:6–16. Why should you be in awe of what God is like?

✢ Read Proverbs 13. Share one of these verses with someone this week.

✢ *Activity:* Watch a sports competition (e.g., an Olympic gymnastics, skating, skateboarding, or snowboarding competition). What do you admire about the athletes? Who made the athletes? Why should you admire God so much more?

Fearing God: What He Is Like—Amazing Love

Have you ever been chosen for something—to have a part in a play or program, put the star on top of the Christmas tree, ride on a float in a parade, win a prize, or something else? What does it feel like to be chosen?

It is great to be chosen by someone to be Joseph or Mary in the Christmas play or to be the pitcher on the baseball team, but think about how much, much greater it is to be chosen by God. No one deserves to be chosen by God! But God did choose people to be His very own special people. He chose Abraham and all his family to become the nation of Israel. Why did He choose them?

> It was not because you were more in number than any other people that the LORD set his love on you and chose you, for you were the fewest of all peoples, but it is because the LORD loves you and is keeping the oath that he swore to your fathers. (Deuteronomy 7:7–8)

Why did God choose Israel to be His people? Is it because they were better than the other nations? Or bigger? No. It was just because the Lord loved them. Israel did not deserve God's love; God just chose to love Israel. It is amazing to be chosen when there is no reason to be chosen.

Amazing is probably what Saul of Tarsus thought when God chose him. There was no reason for God to choose Saul. Saul hated God, and he hated those who loved God. He put Christians in prison and even allowed them to be killed. He was an enemy of God.

On one of his Christian-hating trips, Saul was going to Damascus. He took letters that gave him permission to put any Christians he found there in jail. But on the way,

suddenly a light from heaven shone around him. And falling to the ground he heard a voice saying to him, "Saul, Saul, why are you persecuting me?" (Acts 9:3–4)

Who was speaking to Saul? It was Jesus! He had chosen Saul to be His special preacher to the Gentiles—those who were not Jews. God changed Saul's name to Paul and chose him to be a missionary who preached about Jesus, started churches, and wrote letters to those churches. Those letters Paul wrote became part of the New Testament. The enemy of God had become a child of God. The killer of Christians became a preacher to the lost— to those who don't know God.

What amazing love! God could have killed his enemy, Saul. He could have sent him to hell to suffer forever in torment. Instead, God chose Saul to be a part of His family. What does this tell you about God?

God is an amazing lover of people who don't deserve to be loved. Does that amaze you? Part of what it means to fear the Lord is to be amazed by God's love. Do you know how great His love is?

> For as high as the heavens are above the earth,
>> so great is his steadfast love toward those who fear him.
>>> (Psalm 103:11)

Could you even measure how high the heavens are above the earth? It is so incredibly far that it cannot even be measured. And God's love can't be measured either.

> Know therefore that the LORD your God is God, the faithful God who keeps covenant and steadfast love with those who love him and keep his commandments, to a thousand generations. (Deuteronomy 7:9)

A thousand generations is a long, long time. It is longer than all of history! God will be faithful to His children, and their children, and their children, and their children . . . a thousand times!

Would you like to be chosen by God to receive His amazing love? If you are not a child of God, ask Him to make you a part of His family. He loves all those who belong to Him with a never-ending love. Trust in Jesus, who will make you a child of God.

> But to all who did receive him, who believed in his name, he gave the right to become children of God. (John 1:12)

> See what kind of love the Father has given to us, that we should be called children of God; and so we are. (1 John 3:1)

LEARNING TO TRUST GOD

✢ Read the story of God's amazing love for Saul in Acts 8:1–3, 9:1–19. Where do you see God's amazing love in this story?

✢ Read Proverbs 14. Do you love the wisdom of these proverbs? If you fear the Lord, His words in Proverbs will be a warning to you and will help you to walk in the way of the wise. Make a picture illustrating one of the verses in this chapter.

✢ *Activity:* Mom or Dad, share about a time when you were especially amazed at the love of God for you. As a family, do a loving deed for another person or family so they can see the love of God in you (e.g., make a meal, rake their leaves, visit a lonely older person, clean their house, babysit the children).

Imitating God

Have you ever wanted two different things at the same time—like both ice cream and a chocolate chip cookie for dessert? Part of you wants ice cream and the other part wants the cookie. Your heart is not fully for one thing—it is divided. This is called having a "divided heart."

A divided heart isn't so bad when it comes to dessert, but it is very serious when it comes to faith. To learn the fear of the Lord, you must have an undivided heart toward God. Your heart must be wholly for God, not just partly for God. With all your heart you must be in awe of who God is, admire what He is like, and be amazed at His love. Only God can give you a heart like that:

> Teach me your way, O Lord,
>   that I may walk in your truth;
>   unite my heart to fear your name. (Psalm 86:11)

Because we are born from Adam, we have a sin nature that gives us a divided heart. We want to love God, but we also love the things of the world. We want to serve God, but we also want our own way. We want to walk in the way of the wise, but often our hearts draw us to the way of the foolish.

We cannot get an undivided heart just from trying hard. The only way we can have an undivided heart is if God gives us one. So we must ask God for an undivided heart—for a heart that fears Him and makes Him most important in our lives.

> Teach me your way, O Lord,
>   that I may walk in your truth;
>   unite my heart to fear your name. (Psalm 86:11)

This verse is a prayer that God would teach us to love what is good and right and do those things, and that we would fear Him—be in awe of who He is, admire what He is like, and be amazed at His love. If we truly see who God is and what He is like, we will love Him with a united heart—with an undivided heart.

How does God answer that prayer? Well, do you know what oxen are? Oxen are like cows—only bigger and stronger. Before there were tractors, plows were pulled by oxen. Two oxen were paired together as a team. They were hitched together by a wooden *yoke*, which was like two collars connected together. The yoke kept the two oxen together, and the farmer could "steer" or guide the oxen with his reins and the yoke.

A young ox who didn't know how to pull a plow was put in a yoke with an older ox. The older ox helped the young ox to learn to walk with a yoke, pull a plow, work as a team, and obey the farmer's commands.

This is the same way we can learn the fear of the Lord and the way of wisdom. We can learn from people who are wiser than we are—people who love what is good and right and who do it. But even better, we can learn to walk in the way of the wise from God, who is most wise. If we love God, we will learn to love what He loves. We will learn the way of wisdom because God loves wisdom.

Have you ever played with a baby? How does a baby learn to clap? He watches you. He tries to clap. You show him again, and he tries again. Then one day he is clapping! And you are cheering! This is called "imitation." The baby imitates or follows what you do.

This is the way it is with God and His children. He shows us how to walk in the way of the wise. He loves what is good and right, and all that He does is good and right. When you read the Bible, look for what God loves and what God does. How does He act toward His people? Does He keep His promises? Is He faithful? How does God act toward evil? What do His actions say about His heart? God is the perfect example of walking in wisdom.

We want to be like the people we admire. As we see who God is and what He is like in the Bible, what He loves and how He acts, we should want to be like Him. To learn to walk in God's ways and have a united heart, we must watch and be willing to follow God. We need to look to our heavenly Father and imitate Him.

No matter what you are doing, you can always look to God to teach you what is good and right. But you must have a teachable heart, wanting to do what is good and right. Just stop and pray,

> Teach me your way, O Lord,
>   that I may walk in your truth;
>   unite my heart to fear your name. (Psalm 86:11)

Imagine that someone says something mean to you or something unkind about you. Perhaps the next day this same person wants your help with something. What should you do?

You can ask God to show you what is good and right and to help you do what is wise. How did Jesus act when His friend, Peter, denied Him? He forgave Peter. Maybe God will remind you of this verse:

Beloved, do not imitate evil but imitate good. Whoever does good is from God; whoever does evil has not seen God. (3 John 11)

Now you know what is right to do. If you are a child of God, you can ask God to give you a heart to forgive someone who has hurt you. Then imitate your Father. Learn to walk in His ways as you pray,

Teach me your way, O Lord,
    that I may walk in your truth;
    unite my heart to fear your name. (Psalm 86:11)

LEARNING TO TRUST GOD

✢ Read about the blind beggar and about Zacchaeus in Luke 18:35–19:10. What does this tell you about Jesus? How can you imitate Him?

✢ Read Proverbs 15. What are some of the things God loves? What does this tell you about God?

✢ *Activity:* Learn the art of imitation. Mom or Dad, teach your child how to do something—e.g., sew on a button, bake a cake, crochet a scarf, tie a tie, change a tire, do laundry. Talk about what heart attitudes are important in order to learn by imitation. How can your child learn from God? Pray that you will all have teachable hearts.

The Wise Seek Knowledge

Have you ever gotten a new game you didn't know how to play? Did you just guess how to play the game or make up your own rules? Did you throw it away because you didn't understand the game? What must you do to learn to play a new game? You must read the instructions and learn the rules. Do you know what the Bible says about this?

> An intelligent heart acquires knowledge,
>   and the ear of the wise seeks knowledge. (Proverbs 18:15)

The wise person has a heart that wants to learn. He loves understanding things, so he gets knowledge. He is not lazy, but he works to understand things. A wise person is eager to be taught and to learn. He is humble, knowing that he has much to learn. He knows that wisdom is calling, and he must pay attention to it; he must seek it.

Look around the room you are in. What do you see? Now look again. This time look for rectangles. What are some of the rectangles you see? Did you notice them before? Why not? You were not looking for rectangles at first, so you didn't see them. But once you started to look for rectangles you found them.

If you train yourself to look for wisdom, you will find wisdom, too. That is what it means to "seek wisdom." You have to look for wisdom on purpose.

The foolish person is not like this. In his heart he thinks he knows enough. He is proud and not willing to be taught. He doesn't look for wisdom because he doesn't have the heart to learn.

The Bible tells us about a man who asked Jesus a lot of questions. Nicodemus was an important man, a ruler of the Jews. He knew that God was with Jesus because of all the miracles Jesus did. So Nicodemus was curious about Jesus.

Jesus answered him, "Truly, truly, I say to you, unless one is born again he cannot see the kingdom of God." (John 3:3)

Born again? That sounds strange, doesn't it! It was strange to Nicodemus too. He didn't understand it at all.

Nicodemus said to him, "How can a man be born when he is old? Can he enter a second time into his mother's womb and be born?" (John 3:4)

Jesus told Nicodemus that He wasn't talking about being born as a baby, but about being born spiritually—about trusting in Jesus and having a new heart.

Nicodemus said to him, "How can these things be?" (John 3:9)

Nicodemus was still asking questions. What kind of person was Nicodemus? He wanted to learn. He was seeking knowledge. But to know if he was truly wise, we must know how Nicodemus responded to Jesus' teaching. What did he do about what he heard?

Nicodemus could have been foolish and prideful. He could have hardened his heart and thought that what Jesus said was wrong. He could have decided that he didn't like Jesus' teaching and didn't care about being "born again."

Or he could have been wise and loved what he heard. He could have decided to trust Jesus, follow Him, and believe what Jesus said about being born again. Remember, it is not enough to *know* what is true and right; you must also *do* it.

The Bible gives us a hint about Nicodemus. After Jesus died, a follower of Jesus named Joseph of Arimathea asked if he could bury Jesus' body. Do you know who helped him? Nicodemus.[1] So Nicodemus probably was a follower of Jesus. He probably heard what Jesus said about being born again and trusted Jesus as his Savior. If he did, he was a very wise man.

Unlike Nicodemus, a fool does not seek knowledge and understanding. A fool thinks he already has all the answers. He does not ask many questions or want to learn from someone else.

> A fool takes no pleasure in understanding,
> > but only in expressing his opinion. (Proverbs 18:2)

A person who seeks understanding does not stubbornly try to prove that he is right without listening to the other person. He tries to understand how the other person is thinking, and he asks questions like, "Why do you think that?" or "Can you help me understand what you mean?"

A person who seeks knowledge doesn't think he knows everything, but listens to the instructions of others. He doesn't get mad when someone corrects him, but is glad to learn the right way to do something.

A person who seeks knowledge and understanding does not answer harshly when someone is upset with him. Instead he tries to learn why the other person

---

[1]. See John 19:39.

is upset and asks questions like, "Is something bothering you?" or "Did I say something to offend you?"

A person who seeks knowledge and understanding works at reading and understanding the Bible. Instead of skipping over parts he doesn't understand, he prays for understanding and tries to figure out what it means. Sometimes he asks for help.

Are you this kind of person?

> An intelligent heart acquires knowledge,
> and the ear of the wise seeks knowledge. (Proverbs 18:15)

LEARNING TO TRUST GOD

✣ Read about Nicodemus in John 3:1–15. Ask for help to try to understand this story.

✣ Read Proverbs 16. What does it teach you about the wise person and the foolish person?

✣ *Activity:* Learn a new game. Read the instructions first! What does your attitude about learning the rules of this new game tell you about your heart?

The Wise Love God's Commands

Do you like bread crusts? Some kids don't like them. Suppose you don't like them and you have finished your dinner—except for your bread crust. Hmmm. . . . There is a problem because you *do* like chocolate cake, which is what your mother made for dessert. You can have a piece of cake . . . but only if you finish all your dinner, including your bread crusts.

Eating the cake is easy. You like cake. It is a *delight* to eat it! But eating the crust is not so easy. You eat it because you have to. It is a *duty*—something you *have* to do, not something you necessarily like to do.

God's commands can be like that, too. They can be either a duty for you to obey, or a delight. What makes the difference? They are a duty if your heart does not want to follow what is good and right, but a delight if you love the way of wisdom.

How do you think this writer of the Psalms felt about God's commands?

> Blessed are you, O Lord;
>   teach me your statutes!
> With my lips I declare
>   all the rules of your mouth.
> In the way of your testimonies I delight
>   as much as in all riches.
> I will meditate on your precepts
>   and fix my eyes on your ways.
> I will delight in your statutes;
>   I will not forget your word. (Psalm 119:12–16)

Would you say that he delights to learn, tell about, think about, follow, and obey God's ways, or is it a duty for him? Does he love the way of wisdom, or does he feel forced to walk in the way of wisdom? How do you know this?

A wise person delights in God's ways, in the path of wisdom. In his heart, he wants to turn from what is wrong and do what is right. The Bible says this kind of person is blessed or happy.

> Praise the Lord!
> Blessed is the man who fears the Lord,
>   who greatly delights in his commandments! (Psalm 112:1)

He is happy because he loves what God loves. He knows that following the commands of God brings the greatest happiness. Do you delight in God's commands? Do you love the way of wisdom? The Bible tells us how wonderful God's commands are. It shows us the reason the man has so much joy; it is because he loves the things that God says are good and right:

> My soul melts away for sorrow;
> strengthen me according to your word! (Psalm 119:28)
>
> When I think of your rules from of old,
>   I take comfort, O Lord. (Psalm 119:52)

God's Word strengthens and comforts His children when things are hard. God's Word encourages them. It also helps them to know what is right to do. We don't have to guess what is right; God's Word tells us the way of wisdom that brings true joy and delight.

> Your word is a lamp to my feet
>   and a light to my path. (Psalm 119:105)

> The unfolding of your words gives light;
>   it imparts understanding to the simple. (Psalm 119:130)

God's wise commands keep the hearts of His children from sin. Walking in the way of wisdom keeps them from getting sucked down into the drain of sin after sin after sin that leads to destruction. We can know that all is well with our souls if we delight in God and in his commands for walking in the path of wisdom.

> Keep steady my steps according to your promise,
>   and let no iniquity get dominion over me. (Psalm 119:133)

> Great peace have those who love your law;
>   nothing can make them stumble. (Psalm 119:165)

Your parents can test you on your math facts to see if you know them. But it is harder for them to test your heart to know whether God's commands are a duty or a delight for you. Do you do what is right because you *have* to or because you *want* to? Are God's ways like dry bread crusts to you or like delicious cake?

If you don't like bread crusts, you can make yourself eat them. But you can't make yourself delight in them. It is the same way with God's commands. We can make ourselves do what is right, but we can't make ourselves love what is right. Only God can do that for you. Only God can help you see the goodness of His commands. Only God can make your heart delight in following His commands. All you can do is fill your mind with God's Word and pray that He will put it in your heart.

> Open my eyes, that I may
> > behold wondrous things out of your law. (Psalm 119:18)

> Incline my heart to your testimonies,
> > and not to selfish gain! (Psalm 119:36)

LEARNING TO TRUST GOD

✢ Read Psalm 119:17–24 and 33–40. Do you feel the delight that the psalmist has in God's law? Pray Psalm 119 verses 18 and 36 for yourself every day this week.

✢ Read Proverbs 17. Do you delight in God's wisdom in this chapter? Choose a verse to "test" this week—obey it and see if God's ways bring you delight.

✢ *Activity:* Read Psalm 119:103. As a family, go out for ice cream or have a special family treat and talk about how God's words are sweeter than honey.

The Wise Hate Evil

Does your dad **ever** make a U-turn when he is driving? Why does he do this? He does it when he is going the wrong way. He needs to turn around and go in a different direction.

The wise person also makes U-turns. When he is headed for the path of foolishness, he quickly makes a U-turn. He turns away from what is wrong. He runs from evil. Because he fears the Lord, and because he loves and respects God and knows that God's ways are good and right, he does not want to walk on the path of foolishness.

> Behold, the fear of the Lord, that is wisdom,
> and to turn away from evil is understanding. (Job 28:28)

But the fool is not like the wise person at all. He doesn't turn away from evil.

> One who is wise is cautious and turns away from evil,
> but a fool is reckless and careless. (Proverbs 14:16)

The fool walks right into evil. He is reckless and careless—he doesn't think ahead to the consequences of his actions. He doesn't stop and ask God for help. He is simple, rebellious, and willing to risk destruction.

If a wise person found a book of not very nice jokes in the library, what would he do? He would make a U-turn. He would put it right back, because he hates evil. He wouldn't even look through it. That is running from what is bad and wrong. But the fool wouldn't make a U-turn from evil. What would a fool do?

He would open the book and start reading it. In his heart he would be saying, "Wow! Look what I found. There might be some funny jokes in this book. No one needs to know that I looked at it. Reading a few bad jokes and looking at a few bad pictures isn't going to hurt me. I can handle it." What a foolish thing to do!

If a friend told a fool not to look at the book, what would a fool do? Unlike a wise person who would listen to the good advice of his friend, a fool would ignore it or argue with his friend. He might get mad and tell his friend to mind his own business. That is what the Bible means when it says that a fool is reckless and careless. He doesn't think about consequences or what the bad jokes and pictures would do to his mind and heart. He just jumps into what is wrong.

Do you know why the fool does this? It is because in his heart he doesn't love what is good and right. But a wise person runs away from what is wrong immediately because he hates what is evil. Stopping to wonder if it will really hurt you and thinking about doing it for a while makes it harder to make a U-turn. It is better to turn away as soon as you realize that something is wrong. Can you snap your fingers? The time it takes you to snap your fingers is how fast you should turn from what is wrong.

That is what Joseph did in the book of Genesis. After his brothers sold him into slavery, Joseph was a trusted servant in the house of a man named

Potiphar. Potiphar put Joseph in charge of everything in his house and everything he owned.

But there was a problem. The problem was Potiphar's wife. Joseph was handsome, and Potiphar's wife noticed this. She wanted Joseph to treat her as only a husband should treat a wife. Even though Joseph was in charge of all that Potiphar had, Potiphar's wife was not Joseph's wife.

But God was with Joseph and had given him a wise heart. Joseph knew that what Potiphar's wife asked him to do was wrong and unwise. So he refused to do what she asked. He turned to run from her, but she grabbed his coat-like cloak. Do you know what Joseph did then? He threw off the cloak and ran! He made a U-turn from wrong as fast as you can snap your fingers, and he got far away from evil. A wise man hates evil and runs, runs, runs from it.

It is always right to turn from evil, even if other people don't agree with you or understand . . . or if things don't turn out the way you think they should. Joseph was put in jail because Potiphar's wife lied about him. But still, he knew he had done the right thing and that God was pleased with him. He knew he was on the way of the wise, and he feared the Lord. And eventually he was put in charge of all Egypt.

Do you run from what is wrong? When you are tempted to do something wrong, remember to snap your fingers and get out of there! Do a U-turn!

The fear of the Lord is hatred of evil. (Proverbs 8:13)

LEARNING TO TRUST GOD

✦ Read about Jesus in the temple in John 2:13–17. Why did Jesus overturn the tables and scatter the coins and animals? What was in His heart?

✦ Read Proverbs 18. What does this chapter say about our words? Find one verse to memorize.

✦ *Activity:* The wise man hates evil because he fears God. There is much God-offending evil in our world. What is one thing your family can do to oppose what is wrong? (Suggestions: get involved in a pro-life activity, write a letter to a legislator, pray for a Christian who is imprisoned for his faith.[1])

---

1. See, for example, The Voice of the Martyrs's website: http://www.persecution.com.

The Wise Listen to Advice

Have you ever seen a sign that says, "High Voltage"? Do you know what it means? It is a sign warning people to stay away because there is strong electricity nearby. If you don't want to risk getting killed, you will stay away.

A "high voltage" sign, or a sign that says, "stay off" or "thin ice," gives good advice. It says, "Stay away or you might get hurt." But the sign can only give good advice. It is up to the person to decide whether he will follow or ignore it.

The Bible gives us a command about how to respond to good advice and instruction:

> Listen to advice and accept instruction,
> that you may gain wisdom in the future. (Proverbs 19:20)

When the Bible tells us to "listen" to good advice, does it mean just to "hear" it? What does it mean? It means to obey it—not just to listen to it, but to accept it and follow it. Remember, the wise person knows what is good and right . . . and he *does* it.

David in the Bible was wise like that. He loved God, and he loved what is good and right. So he listened to wise counsel. Do you want to hear the story?

David sent ten of his men to Nabal to ask for a favor. David needed food for his fighting men. It would seem that Nabal would be happy to help David because David had helped Nabal before. But instead of returning kindness for David's kindness, Nabal refused to help David. Nabal was a fool, and he insulted David.

How do you think David felt about that? David was very angry at Nabal and decided to attack Nabal and his men. David wanted to kill Nabal, but that desire was not good and right. It was wrong. David had anger in his heart instead of forgiveness.

God knew that David was about to do a foolish thing. He also knew that David was not a fool. David was a wise man who was tempted to do something wrong. So God sent one of Nabal's servants to warn Nabal's wife, Abigail, of what David was planning to do.

Abigail was a wise woman. Do you know what she did? She sent food to David and admitted that her husband, Nabal, was a fool. She also gave David some good advice. She encouraged David not to take revenge and pay Nabal back for his unkindness, but to let God repay Nabal for his foolishness. God was warning and giving good advice to David through Abigail. Isn't God good to His children?

David was not a fool. He feared God, and he listened to the good advice God sent to him. A fool would have been "reckless and careless" and would have continued to follow the path of foolishness. But David was wise and turned away from evil. He listened to advice and accepted instruction.

The more a person follows good advice, the wiser he becomes. He "gains wisdom in the future." Where can you find good advice? The Bible has the best advice, because it is wisdom from God. But godly parents and other Christians also have good advice for you.

However, not all advice is godly wisdom. Sometimes people give you bad suggestions. Good advice points a person toward God and what is good and right. But bad suggestions point a person toward what is wrong.

Rehoboam was the king of Israel after Solomon died. He got both good advice and a bad suggestion. Which do you think he followed? Solomon made the people of Israel work too hard. But now Israel had a new king and things could be different. So Jeroboam, Solomon's servant, and the people of Israel made a request to Rehoboam:

> Your father made our yoke heavy. Now therefore lighten the hard service of your father and his heavy yoke on us, and we will serve you. (1 Kings 12:4)

Was that a fair request? Yes it was. But Rehoboam wanted to think about it for three days and get some advice. So he asked the older men who had counseled his father for advice. Do you know what they told him?

> If you will be a servant to this people today and serve them, and speak good words to them when you answer them, then they will be your servants forever. (1 Kings 12:7)

Was that good advice? Yes, it was. But instead of listening to the good advice of the older men, Rehoboam took the bad suggestion of his younger friends. They told Rehoboam that he should make things *harder* for the Israelites and make them work more! This made the people of Israel mad . . . and it made them not want to be ruled by Rehoboam.

Following the foolish suggestion of his friends brought a big consequence to Rehoboam. Ten of the twelve tribes of Israel rebelled against Rehoboam and made Jeroboam their king. So, in the end, Rehoboam lost most of his kingdom.

A simple fool follows suggestions without stopping to consider whether they are good or not. A rebellious fool is stubborn and prideful and won't listen to good advice. A mocking fool makes fun of good advice. And the godless fool doesn't care about what God says is good and right. But the wise person knows:

> The way of a fool is right in his own eyes,
> but a wise man listens to advice. (Proverbs 12:15)

LEARNING TO TRUST GOD

✦ Read about how God saved David from foolishness with the good advice of Abigail in 1 Samuel 25. Has God ever saved you from foolishness with good advice from someone?

✦ Read Proverbs 19. What good advice do you see in this chapter? Do you see any bad advice?

✦ *Activity:* As a family, make an acrostic of good advice using the letters of the word PROVERBS.[1] Work in pairs or individually. Then share your words of advice with each other and tell why it is wise counsel.

---

1. For example: Pray about everything; Read your Bible every day; Open your eyes to the beauty in God's world; Vow to be faithful to God every day; Eat healthy food . . . and so on.

The Wise Accept Correction

If you were walking on a path near the edge of a cliff and started to walk off the path, what would your mother and father do? They would tell you to get back on the path or gently pull you back.

Do you know that God does the same thing for His children? God knows how awful and dangerous the way of the foolish is. When His children start to wander off the way of the wise, He rescues them by disciplining them.

Sometimes God's discipline can be gentle. It can be just a little correction—maybe through a verse in the Bible or through a reminder of what is good and right from another person. It can also be a word of "reproof," which is a reprimand or scolding, a firm word of discipline. Can you think of a time when you were corrected or scolded?

Sometimes God's discipline comes as punishment. It can come to His children through parents or other people. Other times it comes through experiencing the consequences of their actions like getting a stomachache from eating too much candy.

If you are a child of God, you will be glad when your parents or God discipline you to keep you on the way of the wise. Maybe you won't be glad right at first, but you will be after a while. In your heart, you will not want to do what is wrong or bad. You know that the way of wisdom is life-giving—it brings joy in this life and eternal life and joy in heaven.

> The ear that listens to life-giving reproof
>   will dwell among the wise.
> Whoever ignores instruction despises himself,
>   but he who listens to reproof gains intelligence.
>   (Proverbs 15:31–32)

But if you are not a child of God and you do not love the way of wisdom, you will be angry when you are disciplined, and you will stay angry. The problem is not just doing the wrong things. The bigger problem is the wrong attitudes and desires in the heart. Hating God's discipline and not turning away from foolishness will lead to destruction.

> There is severe discipline for him who forsakes the way;
> whoever hates reproof will die. (Proverbs 15:10)

Are you ready to hear another story about David? In this story, David was disciplined by God because David did something very wrong. King David took another man's wife and treated her like his own wife. That was a terrible sin. But then, to cover up that sin, David did something else very evil. He had the woman's husband, Uriah, killed in battle so that no one would know that he had taken Uriah's wife, Bathsheba.

But someone did know, and that someone was God, who knows everything. David thought his foolishness was hidden from everyone, but nothing is ever hidden from God. Even though David did some very wrong things and had sin in his heart, he was still a child of God and loved God.

God loves His children—even when they sin. Because He loves them, He does not allow His children to continue down the path of foolishness. What did God do about David's sin?

God sent a prophet named Nathan to discipline and correct David. God used Nathan to help David see his sin so David would repent. David had a choice. He could "listen to life-giving reproof" and accept correction, or he could ignore or even hate God's correction.

David was a wise man who accepted correction because he loved God and what is good and right. He admitted his sin and God was merciful. David was quick to repent and turn back to the way of the wise.

> David said to Nathan, "I have sinned against the Lord." And Nathan said to David, "The Lord also has put away your sin; you shall not die." (2 Samuel 12:13)

God is merciful to His children, but God is also just—He is right in all He does and must punish sin. There needed to be consequences for David to help him to see how serious sin is and how much it offends God.

Why else do you think God brought consequences to David? God knows foolishness or "folly" is in the heart, and "the rod of discipline drives it" out. He punishes His children in order to "unstick" the sin from their hearts. He wants to give them a hatred for what is wrong and a love for what is right, and to keep them on the way of the wise. What a faithful God He is!

He disciplines his children only enough to teach their hearts to love what is right. He loves them so much that He will not let them wander off the way of the wise. That is why the Bible tells us,

My son, do not despise the LORD's discipline
    or be weary of his reproof,
for the LORD reproves him whom he loves,
    as a father the son in whom he delights. (Proverbs 3:11–12)

How do you respond to discipline? Do you listen to "life-giving reproof" and wisely accept correction so you may walk on the way of the wise?

The ear that listens to life-giving reproof
    will dwell among the wise.
Whoever ignores instruction despises himself,
    but he who listens to reproof gains intelligence. (Proverbs 15:31–32)

LEARNING TO TRUST GOD

✣ Read 2 Samuel 12:1–14. Why was Nathan's rebuke a blessing to David? What were the consequences of David's sin? Were they too harsh? Why not? Ask God to give you a wise heart that loves discipline.

✣ Read Proverbs 20. What verse shows that discipline is good for us?

✣ *Activity:* Read Proverbs 29:1. What does it mean to "stiffen" the neck? Mom or Dad, recount a time when you saw this verse come true. Is there someone you know who needs to be warned about walking the way of the foolish? What can your family do to graciously encourage him to walk on the way of the wise? Pray that this person will not continue to "stiffen his neck."

The Wise Have Self-Control

There are two ways of coloring a picture. One is to hurry and be sloppy, going outside the lines and coloring in all directions. Little children color like this. But as they get older, children learn to use more control—coloring more slowly in one direction and being careful not to go outside the lines. What is the difference? The difference is self-control or self-discipline—they learn to hold themselves back and control the desire to finish quickly and be sloppy; they learn to make patient, careful moves.

Self-control is learning to control yourself or hold yourself back, and it is a good thing. Those who walk in wisdom have self-control.

> A fool gives full vent to his spirit,
> but a wise man quietly holds it back. (Proverbs 29:11)

The wise man "keeps himself under control."[1] He doesn't quickly jump into things, but he is careful and thoughtful about his actions. The wise person shows self-control in many ways—in his words, his emotions, his eating, the way he spends money . . . in all things. Instead of bursting out in anger, a wise person tries to understand the other person. Rather than foolishly spending his money on whatever he happens to see and want, the wise person is thoughtful about how he will use his money. He carefully makes a wise buying choice, or saves his money until he has enough to buy something worthwhile.

The Bible has a lot to say about wise men and self-control:

> It is an honor for a man to keep aloof from strife,
> but every fool will be quarreling. (Proverbs 20:3)

---

1. Proverbs 29:11, NIV.

Fools carelessly jump into arguments, but the wise person thinks carefully about what to say and how to say it.

> Precious treasure and oil are in a wise man's dwelling,
>   but a foolish man devours it. (Proverbs 21:20)

The fool doesn't think about tomorrow or what he will need then. He uses whatever he wants for today . . . even if there is nothing left over for tomorrow.

If a fool were given a bag of candy bars, what would he do? He would eat as many as he wants whenever he wants, having no self-control. If he wants to do it, he does it. He might even eat three candy bars at a time.

What would the wise person do? He would be thoughtful and wise about eating the candy bars. He realizes that they are not healthy and would eat one once in a while; he might even give some away. The wise person acts slowly and thoughtfully.

This is what King David did. His son, Absalom, turned people against David and tried to make himself king in David's place. So David had to run away from the royal city of Jerusalem. As he was escaping, Shimei, a man from the family of David's old enemy, Saul, cursed him—saying all kinds of bad things to him—and threw rocks at him and his officials. But David's army of fighting men was with him.

> Then Abishai the son of Zeruiah said to the king, "Why should this dead dog curse my lord the king? Let me go over and take off his head." (2 Samuel 16:9)

What answer would a foolish man give Abishai? A fool would become angry and, without thinking, do something to Shimei. He would not have the self-control to wisely keep moving. But David wasn't a fool. He was thoughtful and careful. He decided how he would handle the situation instead of just jumping in and doing something.

> And David said to Abishai and to all his servants, "Behold, my own son seeks my life; how much more now may this Benjaminite! Leave him alone, and let him curse, for the Lord has told him to. It may be that the

> Lord will look on the wrong done to me, and that the Lord will repay me with good for his cursing today." So David and his men went on the road, while Shimei went along on the hillside opposite him and cursed as he went and threw stones at him and flung dust. (2 Samuel 16:11–13)

How much self-control did it take for David to leave Shimei alone and let the Lord take care of Shimei? It must have been very hard. But God helped David.

The wise person gains self-control by learning to "speak to himself" and not to "listen to himself." Speaking to yourself is telling yourself the words of wisdom. The fool listens to himself—"I love candy bars"—and gobbles them up. But the wise person speaks to himself—"Self, I know you like candy bars. But candy bars are not good for you. You don't have to eat three candy bars. You can be content with just one."

Are you learning to have self-control? Are you learning to speak to yourself instead of just listening to yourself?

> Whoever is slow to anger is better than the mighty,
>   and he who rules his spirit than he who takes a city. (Proverbs 16:32)

LEARNING TO TRUST GOD

✤ Read Proverbs 16:32 again. What does it mean to "rule your spirit"? Why is the person with self-control greater than the person who takes a city? (Hint: Which is harder?)

✤ Read Proverbs 21. What does verse 23 teach you about self-control? Verse 25?

✤ *Activity:* Give some examples of listening to yourself and talking to yourself. Copy and color the traffic light picture at the back of this book and use it as a reminder to stop, wait, and go with self-control.

The Wise Look Ahead

Have you ever heard the expression, "Look before you leap"? What does it mean? It means more than just looking where you are jumping before you jump . . . because you might jump into a thornbush or a bee's nest or something else unpleasant. It means that you should think about where your actions will lead you. "Look" before you do something. You should think about the possible consequences of what you are planning to do.

If you don't look at what is ahead you could find yourself in trouble. If you dive into water without first checking to see whether it is safe, you could be surprised, and very hurt if you land on a big rock. That is why it is important to "look before you leap."

The wise person looks ahead before he jumps into something. But the fool doesn't do that. He is "reckless and careless" and doesn't think about the end of his actions. He does whatever comes to his mind without thinking about what could happen.

Jephthah was that kind of person. He was a mighty warrior who was asked to lead Israel in fighting against the Ammonites. He really wanted to win the battle, so he did a very foolish thing. He made a promise to God without thinking about what might happen. He did not look ahead but "leaped without looking."

Guess what he promised?

> Jephthah made a vow to the Lord and said, "If you will give the Ammonites into my hand, then whatever comes out from the doors of my house to meet me when I return in peace from the Ammonites shall be the Lord's, and I will offer it up for a burnt offering." (Judges 11:30–31)

Was it good for Jephthah to promise to offer for a burnt offering whatever came out of his door? What could come out of his door? Let's find out what happened.

God did "give the Ammonites" into Jephthah's hand. Jephthah and his men destroyed twenty towns and defeated the Ammonites.

Then Jephthah came to his home at Mizpah. And behold, his daughter came out to meet him with tambourines and with dances. She was his only child; besides her he had neither son nor daughter. (Judges 11:34)

What a foolish promise Jephthah made! He did not look ahead. He just opened his mouth and spoke foolishly without thinking about the consequences. Jephthah wept over his hasty, foolish vow that would bring such sadness.

"Look before you leap" is a good phrase to learn. It can remind you to look ahead instead of acting foolishly without thinking of the consequences.

> The prudent sees danger and hides himself,
> but the simple go on and suffer for it. (Proverbs 27:12)

A prudent person is a wise person. A wise person keeps away from danger, but a fool walks right into danger without thinking. If we do not look ahead before we act, there can be some very serious consequences. Samson had to learn this lesson.

Do you remember who the Philistines were? They were enemies of Israel. They were afraid of Samson because he was so strong. But Samson was foolish enough to make a close friendship with a Philistine woman named Delilah. Many times Delilah asked Samson the secret of his strength. Each time he made up an answer that was not true, and each time Delilah showed Samson that she could not be trusted.

Still Samson kept going to be with Delilah . . . and one day, Samson told her that the secret of his strength was his long hair. He did not look ahead and think about what his enemies might do if they knew his secret.

When Samson was sleeping, Delilah cut off his hair. So he was not strong enough to fight off the Philistines when they attacked him. The Philistines treated Samson cruelly and made him a slave. Even though Samson knew Delilah could not be trusted, he foolishly kept seeing Delilah and "suffered for it." He didn't run away from danger. He ran right into it without looking ahead and considering the consequences.

The wise person thinks about where his attitudes, choices, and actions will lead. He thinks ahead to what will happen, and is wise about not taking the next step toward a foolish thing. When he thinks about doing something like cheating on a math test, he looks ahead and considers where it might lead.

A wise person thinks about the consequences of cheating. He thinks about the harm to his soul, about maybe getting caught and punished, or about being tempted to lie to cover it up—the things that could happen right away. And he also thinks about the things that could happen after a long time—like not learning math well, starting a habit of cheating, not being trusted by others, or starting down the path of foolishness that leads to destruction.

What about you? How can you learn to "look before you leap"?

The prudent sees danger and hides himself,
> but the simple go on and suffer for it. (Proverbs 27:12)

LEARNING TO TRUST GOD

✢ Read about Samson in Judges 16:6–21. Where do you see Samson following foolish thinking? How did he "go ahead and suffer for it"? Think of some situations. What does "looking ahead" or "looking before you leap" look like in those situations?

✢ Read Proverbs 22. Explain two of the proverbs to someone else.

✢ *Activity:* As a family, make a favorite recipe or work on a simple project without "looking ahead" to see what ingredients/materials are needed.[1] Then look ahead and make a list. Pick up what is lacking at another time and complete your recipe/project. Talk about why looking ahead is wise. Pray that God would give you wise hearts to look ahead to consequences and make wise decisions.

---

1. Make sure you are lacking some of the ingredients.

The Wise Trust God

Sometimes you can stand on your tiptoes to reach something high . . . and you just might reach it if it isn't too high. But sometimes you need something else to stand on because even on your tiptoes, you just can't reach it, even if you stretch really far.

Some things we just can't do by ourselves. We aren't tall enough, strong enough, wise enough, or good enough. We are weak. But God isn't like us—He is more than strong enough, more than wise enough, and more than good enough for everything! He is never weak. He is perfect in all ways. So it is better to trust in God than to trust in ourselves.

Israel had seen so many of God's miracles. Can you imagine what it must have been like to be one of the tribes of Israel—like the Ephraimites? Just think of all that God did for them. Surely they knew they could trust Him for everything!

> The Ephraimites, armed with the bow,
> > turned back on the day of battle.
> They did not keep God's covenant,
> > but refused to walk according to his law.
> They forgot his works
> > and the wonders that he had shown them. (Psalm 78:9–11)

Israel didn't think about God's miracles: how He had split the sea so they could walk across to safety, led them in the wilderness with the cloud and pillar of fire, and caused water to gush from the rocks to quench their thirst in the desert. He was so good to them, taking care of them, protecting them, and providing for them.

Yet they sinned still more against him,
    rebelling against the Most High in the desert.
. . . .
They did not believe in God
    and did not trust his saving power. (Psalm 78:17, 22)

Isn't this a sad story? God had done so many miracles for Israel, and yet His people did not trust Him to give them food in the wilderness. Was that any harder for God than the miracles He had already done? The Israelites should have trusted God, but they doubted that He could "spread a table in the wilderness"—that He could give them food.

Why couldn't the Israelites trust God? They were looking at the bigness of their problem . . . not the greatness of God. They should have remembered who God is, what He is like, and what He had done for them. But they didn't.

If the Israelites could fail to trust God, so can we. Do you remember the story Jesus told about the two houses with different foundations, one of sand and one of rock? The first step in trusting God is to trust in Jesus, the Rock, as your sure foundation. If you are not first trusting Jesus to turn away God's anger at your sin, you cannot trust God to work for your good, because you are not His child. But if you are trusting in Jesus as your Savior, God will help you in every situation if you trust in Him.

> Trust in the Lord with all your heart,
> 	and do not lean on your own understanding.
> In all your ways acknowledge him,
> 	and he will make straight your paths. (Proverbs 3:5–6)

God will make your paths straight! Do you know what that means? Is it easier to follow a straight path or a winding path? When the Bible talks about your path being straight, it means a good, clear path. "He will make straight your paths" means that God will help you walk in the way of the wise. You will know what is right and good, and you will do it. If you trust in God rather than in yourself, you will be strong and not easily shaken. You will not easily stray off the way of the wise.

This verse also tells us something we must do for God to make our paths straight. What is it? We must trust in the Lord instead of leaning on our "own understanding." Leaning on our own understanding is depending on ourselves. It is trusting that our own wisdom is enough for us to make good choices.

But we do not have enough understanding to always make wise decisions. We don't know what will happen tomorrow, or what other people will do. There are many things we don't understand or can't know. To trust in ourselves is as foolish as trusting a foundation of sand.

Only God knows all things—He knows what will happen tomorrow, next week, and next year; He knows everything about our situation, what other people will do, and what their decisions will mean for us. He knows what is best. We can only guess at these things. We cannot lean on our own understanding, because our understanding is not enough. God's understanding is more than enough.

If we cannot lean on our own understanding, what can we do?

> Trust in the Lord with all your heart,
>> and do not lean on your own understanding.
> In all your ways acknowledge him,
>> and he will make straight your paths. (Proverbs 3:5–6)

If you said, *"in all your ways acknowledge"* God, you are right! In everything, even the things that we think we know, we need to ask God to show us what is right. We need to ask God for wisdom instead of thinking we know the answers ourselves. We need to ask Him for the strength to do what is right. We need to depend on God instead of ourselves.

How can you learn to trust God more?

> Those who trust in the Lord are like Mount Zion,
>> which cannot be moved, but abides forever.
> As the mountains surround Jerusalem,
>> so the Lord surrounds his people,
>> from this time forth and forevermore. (Psalm 125:1–2)

LEARNING TO TRUST GOD

✦ Read 2 Corinthians 1:8–11. Why does hardship and suffering teach us to rely on God? What kind of help does Paul ask for? Do you know of anyone going through a hard time? Ask God to help this person trust in Him.

✦ Read Proverbs 23. What does this tell you about trusting in riches, discipline, and your parents' instruction?

✦ *Activity:* Set up an obstacle course. Take turns being blindfolded and trusting someone else to lead you through the course. What does it look like to trust that person? What must you do?

The End of the Path

If you were going on a trip, would you rather travel in an airplane or a bus? An airplane is comfortable and fast, and you get a snack and something to drink. But on a bus . . . well, you get a seat and a long ride. And no one serves snacks and drinks on a bus!

So you would probably say that you would rather go on a plane. But first you need to know where the plane and the bus are going. Suppose the plane is going to the desert where it's hot and there is no food or water. The bus is slow and the trip is long, but it's going to Disneyland where there are so many fun and interesting things to do. So now, would you choose the plane or the bus?

Life is very much like a trip. If you are walking on the way of the wise with Jesus as your sure foundation, you are on your way to heaven. There are bumps in the road, and sometimes you get hurt and life is uncomfortable or even painful. But where you are going is a zillion times better than Disneyland! You are on your way to heaven, where there are no tears or sickness and there will be dancing and rejoicing, because you will be enjoying the King of Kings, the God of the whole universe, your Friend and Savior, Jesus.

Sometimes when we see someone walking the way of the foolish, life can look pretty good for him. Maybe he has more money than us or fewer troubles, has more friends, or is smarter or better at sports. The Bible tells us the truth about the foolish.

> My steps had nearly slipped.
> For I was envious of the arrogant
>   when I saw the prosperity of the wicked.
>
> For they have no pangs until death;
> . . . .

> They are not stricken like the rest of mankind.
> . . . .
> Always at ease, they increase in riches.
> . . . .
>
> But when I thought how to understand this,
>   it seemed to me a wearisome task,
> until I went into the sanctuary of God;
>   then I discerned their end.
>
> Truly you set them in slippery places;
>   you make them fall to ruin.
> How they are destroyed in a moment,
>   swept away utterly by terrors! (Psalm 73:2–5, 12, 16–19)

Sometimes, even though fools—those who love what is wrong and bad—look like they are getting all kinds of good things, they are actually on the path of destruction. Right now they might be "on a plane," comfortable and enjoying good things, but someday they will be suddenly thrown into hell. There will be no way out, like there wasn't for the rich man in the story of Lazarus that Jesus told. Those in hell will be there forever.

Psalm 73 tells us not to be jealous of the fool when he is "on a plane ride" that looks good now, because he is on his way to hell. What does it matter if he enjoys some good things on the trip of life? He is going to a place of suffering and torment forever.

So when you decide which path to follow through life, don't just look at the bumps or the fun things along the way. Be sure you look at the end of the path. Where is it going? Eternal destruction or eternal life?

Jesus told a story about a rich man who gathered so much food from his fields that he did not know where to put it all. So he tore down his barns and built bigger barns. What does this tell you about his heart? He had more than enough, but instead of sharing he decided to keep it all. Even worse, he thought he had so much that he could just take it easy and have a good time with no thought about anything serious.

> But God said to him, "Fool! This night your soul is required of you, and the things you have prepared, whose will they be?" So is the one who lays up treasure for himself and is not rich toward God. (Luke 12:20–21)

Why was this man a fool? He didn't love generosity or what is good and right. He lived his life with no thought for God. He was a godless fool with no room for God.

What happened to his riches when he died? He had to leave his treasure here on earth and had no treasure at the end of his path because God was not his treasure. Life on earth is very short, but where you go will be forever. Like all people, this man died, and all the comfortable things in his life came to a very sudden end.

Would you rather go to a funeral or a party?

> The heart of the wise is in the house of mourning,
>   but the heart of fools is in the house of mirth. (Ecclesiastes 7:4)

Do you know what mirth is? It is fun and laughing. Mourning is sadness and crying. So why would the heart of the wise be in the "house of mourning"? Isn't it better to laugh and have fun at a party than to cry at a funeral?

It's more pleasant to laugh and have fun, but thinking about sin, death, and hell is very important. The wise person realizes that funerals will come for everyone, and in his heart the wise person wants to be ready for death. He wants to be on the path that leads to heaven and eternal life. The good thing about funerals is that they help us think about our own end, the path we are on, and where we are going.

> It is better to go to the house of mourning
> > than to go to the house of feasting,
> for this is the end of all mankind,
> > and the living will lay it to heart. (Ecclesiastes 7:2)

Will you think about what path you are on today?

LEARNING TO TRUST GOD

✦ Read Ecclesiastes 7:2 again. What does "lay it to heart" mean? How can you lay the teaching of this verse and this lesson "to heart"? Do you know what path you are on? How do you know this?

✦ Read Proverbs 24. What does this verse say about the end of the path of the fool?

✦ *Activity:* When we see people walking the path of foolishness, we should feel great sorrow and fear for them, not envy. As a family, think of something you can do to warn someone who is not walking the way of the wise about the end of his path. How can you share the gospel of Jesus with this person? Pray for this person and take a step to share the gospel with him.

Jesus Is the Bridge

Have you ever **played** the game "Who am I?" You are given clues to guess who the person is. Let's play it!

Who am I? I was a king of Israel with great wisdom. I built a very important building and wrote two books of the Bible. Who am I?

If you guessed Solomon, you are right! Solomon was the main writer of the book of Proverbs, which teaches us about wisdom and foolishness. He also built the temple where the people of Israel could worship God. It seems that Solomon must have walked on the way of the wise.

But Solomon was a "contradiction." A contradiction is like an opposite. It can be saying one thing but doing something very different. Although Solomon knew many wise things, he did not act in a wise way. It seems that Solomon's wisdom was only in his head and not in his heart, at least toward the end of his life.[1]

The book of Ecclesiastes helps us to understand the story of Solomon's life. It is the story of not acting wisely and of trying to find happiness in all kinds of things—knowledge, pleasure, wealth, doing important things like building the temple, and being an important king. But none of this brought Solomon true joy. Finally, Solomon discovered something that he knew in his head but had not loved in his heart.

> The end of the matter; all has been heard. Fear God and keep his commandments, for this is the whole duty of man. (Ecclesiastes 12:13)

Do you remember what it means to "fear God"? It means to be in awe of who He is, to admire what He is like, and to be amazed at His love. If we truly see

---

[1]. Although we cannot note with certainty Solomon's eternal destiny, the Bible clearly suggests that he walked a very foolish path even though he possessed great wisdom. See 1 Kings 11:1–13 for an explanation of the foolishness apparent at the end of his life.

who God is and what He is like, we will love Him with an undivided heart. We will want to follow God's commands, and we will walk in the way of the wise because we love what is right and good.

Solomon knew all about fearing God, but he did not truly fear God. He was wise in his head, but not in his heart. Why does the Bible tell us about Solomon?

Solomon's life is a warning that we can know the right things and not love them. We can know about God, and not love or fear God. The Bible—and sometimes even the church—is full of people like Solomon. Because God loves us, God tells us in the Bible about these people so that we will be warned not to be like them.

This is what God said about the stories of rebellious Israel:

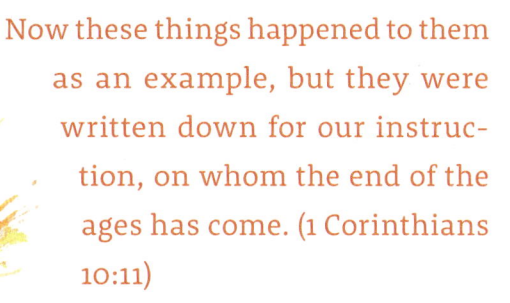

> Now these things happened to them as an example, but they were written down for our instruction, on whom the end of the ages has come. (1 Corinthians 10:11)

God is warning us. You can know what is good and right, but not love or do those things. You can know all about God and not love or follow Him. You can be a contradiction. You can say all the right words, give all the right answers, and quote all kinds of verses, yet your heart can be far from true wisdom and from God. You can be a "pretend Christian."

Wearing a white lab coat doesn't make you a doctor. You might look like one, but you are not a doctor. In the same way, "looking like a Christian" doesn't make someone a Christian. Just because a person *looks* like he is walking the way of the wise doesn't mean that he truly loves what is good and right. He can be trying to do "all the right things," but it might be pretend.

He can read his Bible but not obey it. He can act like he is taking good advice but really be mad about it. He can say he loves God but continually disobey God. If he really doesn't love God or the way of the wise, he is only pretending to be a Christian.

Sodom and Gomorrah were full of fools who loved what is bad and wrong. Lot lived in Sodom but he loved what is good and right. Two angels warned Lot that God would be destroying Sodom and Gomorrah because of the evil, sinful hearts and actions of the people.

Lot was wise and listened to the angels' warning. He took his family and ran away from Sodom. The angels warned them not to look back, but Lot's wife foolishly ignored the warning. She looked back and was turned into a pillar of salt. She was not grateful for God's mercy and did not rejoice in the rescue He was offering. Instead, she looked back at what she was leaving. She set her heart on things of the world instead of on God. This is not walking the way of the wise.

> Do not love the world or the things in the world. If anyone loves the world, the love of the Father is not in him. (1 John 2:15)

Even when her life depended on walking on the way of the wise, Lot's wife could not do it, because her heart was not on the way of the wise. Her heart was in Sodom and Gomorrah, on the way of the foolish. She tried to walk the way of the wise in her own strength, but she couldn't. She wasn't strong enough. She wanted the things of the world.

A person walking on the way of the foolish cannot cross over to the way of the wise by himself. He cannot set his feet on the right path. He will listen to the call of the world, the call of foolishness. His heart will pull him away from the rescue of God. There is only one way to get from the way of the foolish to the way of the wise.

> Jesus said . . . "I am the way, and the truth, and the life. No one comes to the Father except through me." (John 14:6)

Jesus is the only way to God and the way of the wise. We cannot fear God, love his commands, or love what is good and right without trusting in the work of Jesus on the cross to take away our sins, change our hearts, and give us eternal joy.

Are you trusting in Jesus? Are you on the way of the wise?

LEARNING TO TRUST GOD

- Read about Sodom and Gomorrah and Lot's wife in Genesis 18:20–19:1, 12–26. What does this tell you about God's mercy and holiness and the way of the foolish?

- Read Proverbs 25. What does this tell you about the way of foolishness and the way of the wise?

- *Challenge:* Continue reading the book of Proverbs until you finish it.

- *Activity:* Examine a fake plant or flower. Make a long list of the differences between a fake plant or flower and a real one. How does this help you understand the difference between a fake Christian and a real one? Ask God to put the fear of Him in your heart—awe of who He is, admiration for what He is like, and amazement at His love.

CHARACTERISTICS OF THE WISE:
SELF-CONTROLLED

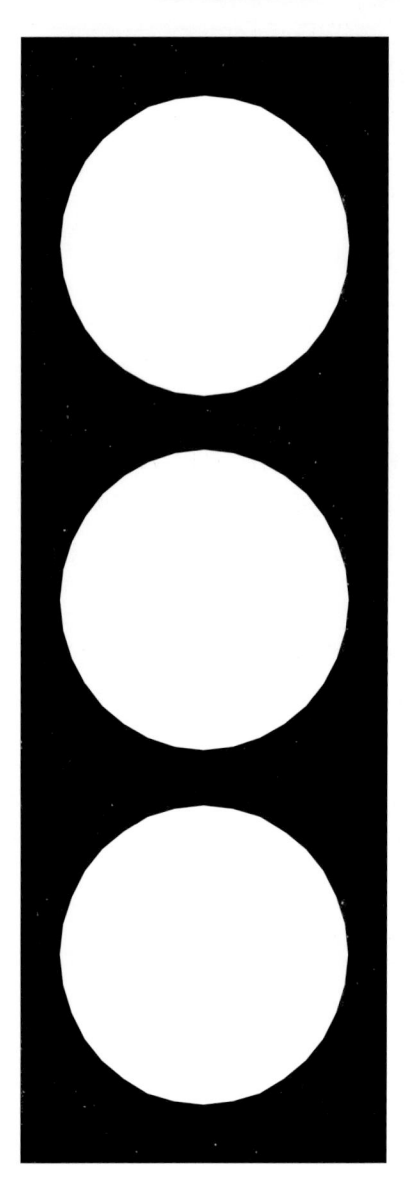

STOP!
Don't listen to your "self"

WAIT!
Think, pray, Decide, and talk to your "self"

GO!
Walk in the Way of the Wise

Color each light the appropriate color; color in the letters, and decorate the borders.

Praise for *God's Wisdom*

Wisdom comes from God's Word. Once again, Sally Michael has used her fervent love for Christ and her keen understanding of the Scriptures to help parents and children to see that fact. I'm very excited to put this book into the hands of parents.

—DEEPAK REJU, Associate Pastor, Capitol Hill Baptist Church, Washington, D.C.

In *God's Wisdom*, Sally Michael seamlessly weaves New Testament and Old Testament stories together to teach biblical wisdom in a way that is clear, fun, and engaging for children. Her compelling word pictures and analogies make difficult concepts easier to grasp. Sally offers our kids more than biblical horse sense; she grounds biblical wisdom in the gospel. Parents looking for tools to point their children to Christ would be wise to buy this book for their family.

—MARTY MACHOWSKI, Pastor, Author of *Long Story Short* and *The Gospel Story Bible*

In the midst of a culture that by its deceptive promises of happiness and success is constantly enticing our children to embrace the folly of sin, Sally provides families with a much needed antidote: *God's Wisdom*. This book is filled with essential biblical wisdom, conveyed in a manner that is wonderfully accessible to children. Additionally, it gives parents numerous practical ideas for applying God's wisdom to the heart and to every area of life.

—JILL NELSON, Curriculum Author, *Children Desiring God*

children desiring God

This storybook was adapted from *The Way of the Wise*, an upper-elementary Sunday school curriculum published by Children Desiring God (CDG). If you would like to further explore the wisdom of God or other aspects of His counsel with your student, resources are available from Children Desiring God.

Children Desiring God is a non-profit ministry that Sally Michael and her husband, David Michael, helped to establish in the late 1990s. CDG publishes God-centered, Bible-saturated, Christ-exalting resources to help parents and churches train their children spiritually in the hope that the next generation will see and embrace Jesus Christ as the one who saves and satisfies the soul. Resources include curriculum for children of nursery age through youth (see sequence chart on following page), parenting booklets, and Bible memory resources. Free parenting and Christian education training audio and video resources are also available online.

Please contact us if we can partner with you for the joy of the next generation.

childrendesiringGOD.org
cdg@desiringGOD.org

	SUNDAY SCHOOL	
Nursery	**A Sure Foundation** A Philosophy and Curriculum for Ministry to Infants and Toddlers	
Preschool	**He Established a Testimony** Old Testament Stories for Young Children	
Preschool	**He Has Spoken By His Son** New Testament Stories for Young Children	

	SUNDAY SCHOOL	MIDWEEK
K	**Jesus, What a Savior!** A Study for Children on Redemption	**He Has Been Clearly Seen** A Study for Children on Seeing and Delighting in God's Glory
1	**The ABCs of God** A Study for Children on the Greatness and Worth of God	**I Stand in Awe** A Study for Children on the Bible
2	**Faithful to All His Promises** A Study for Children on the Promises of God	(Children Desiring God will announce plans for this title in the future.)
3	**In the Beginning . . . Jesus** A Chronological Study for Children on Redemptive History	**The Way of the Wise** A Study for Children on Wisdom and Foolishness
4	**To Be Like Jesus** A Study for Children on Following Jesus	**I Will Build My Church** A Study for Children on the Church (future release)
5	**How Majestic Is Your Name** A Study for Children on the Names and Character of God	**Fight the Good Fight** A Study for Children on Persevering in Faith
6	**My Purpose Will Stand** A Study for Children on the Providence of God	**Pour Out Your Heart Before Him** A Study for Children on Prayer and Praise in the Psalms (future release)
7	**Your Word Is Truth** A Study for Youth on Seeing All of Life through the Truth of Scripture	**Abiding in Jesus** A Study for Youth on Trusting Jesus and Encouraging Others
8	**Teach Me Your Way** A Study for Youth on Surrender to Jesus and Submission to His Way	**Rejoicing in God's Good Design** A Study for Youth on Biblical Manhood and Womanhood

Also by Sally Michael

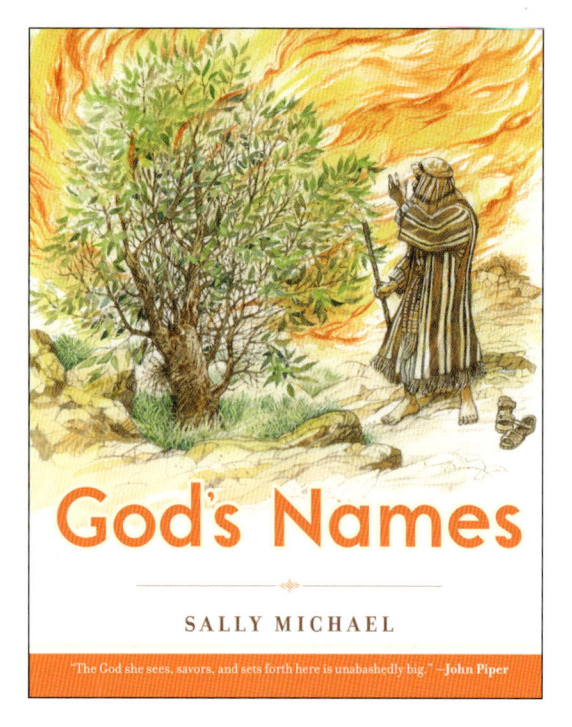

God has left his names with his people so they can know him . . . and through these pages your children can know him too.

"The God she sees, savors, and sets forth here is unabashedly big. Not distant and uncaring. But great enough to make his caring count."
—JOHN PIPER, Pastor for Preaching and Vision, Bethlehem Baptist Church, Minneapolis, MN

"Sally Michael creatively helps parents to lead their children through a fun and fascinating exploration of the various ways God's names reveal the beauty and power of his character and actions."
—JUSTIN TAYLOR, Managing Editor, *ESV Study Bible*

When you want to get to know someone, where do you start? How do you introduce yourself?

Usually you start with someone's name.

God knows this—and he doesn't have just one name to share with us, either! The Bible gives us many names for God and tells us what they all mean. And when we learn a new name for God, we learn something new about him, too!

This book is for you and your children to read together. Every chapter teaches something new and helps put you—and your children—on the right track in your relationship with God.

"Grandparents and parents and all the extended family, as well as those who make up the church of the living God—all have a divine unction to pass along God's truth to the hearts of our children! Sally Michael has given us an excellent tool in *God's Names* to do just that!"
—DOROTHY PATTERSON, General Editor of *The Woman's Study Bible* and Professor of Theology in Woman's Studies, Southwestern Baptist Theological Seminary

Also by Sally Michael

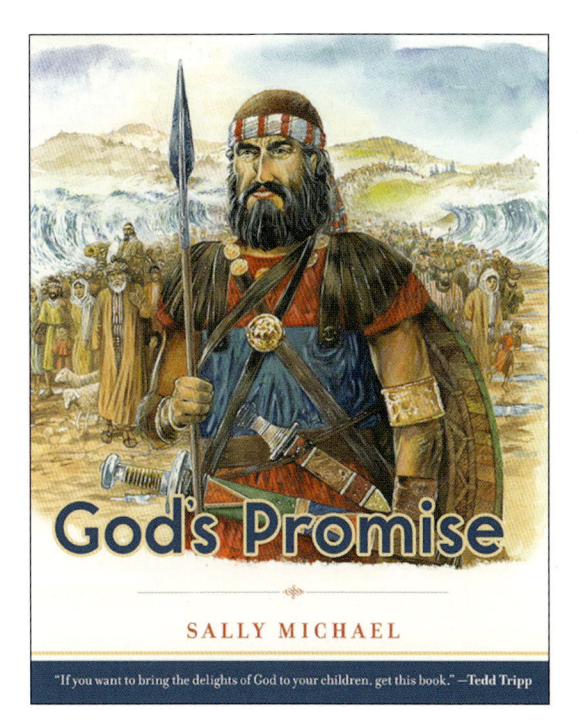

You have probably seen your children's eyes light up at receiving a present.

How excited would they be to get a present directly from God?

God already has a present to offer your children. And you can be the one who helps them discover it.

God has left all of his children many promises through his Word as gifts that flow from his goodness and love. Each one is backed up by his power and trustworthy character, so we can be confident in them.

This book, for you and your children to read together, will help them learn these promises and put their own confidence in them. Each chapter looks at a new promise and explores it in the context of a Bible story.

God has left his promises with his people so they can trust him . . . and through these pages your children can trust him too.

"This engaging, attractively illustrated book teaches not only the promises of the Bible, but also the character of the God who makes and keeps his promises."
—TEDD TRIPP, President of Shepherding the Heart Ministries

"This book is clear, profound, helpful, and at every point grounded with faith and confidence in who God is. A tremendous resource!"
—ELIZABETH GROVES, Lecturer in Old Testament, Westminster Seminary

"Sally Michael does not sugarcoat any of the more difficult promises, but explains them in a way that shows a high view of God. . . . I highly recommend it."
—MARTHA PEACE, Biblical Counselor, Co-author of *The Faithful Parent*

Also by Sally Michael

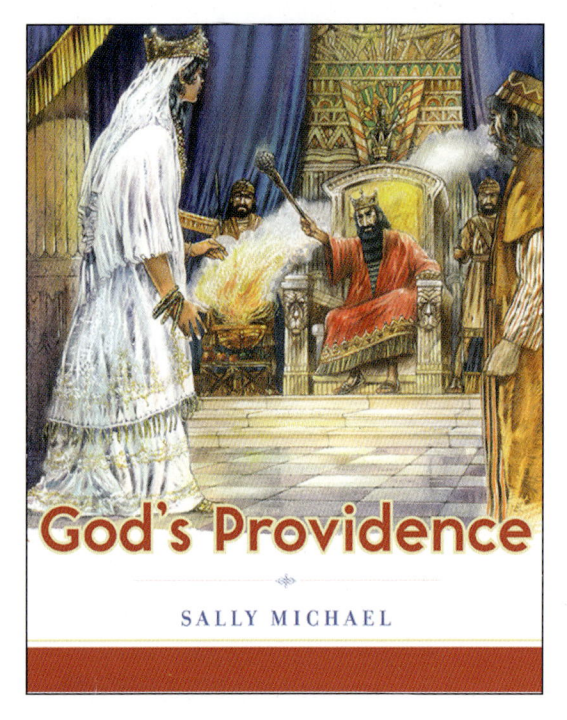

All parents want their children to feel secure.

How reassuring would it be for your child to know that nothing is outside God's control?

Every person, every circumstance, and every action is part of God's plan—a plan that works all things for the good of those who love him. This is God's providence, a doctrine that brings us joy even as it staggers our understanding.

Can a child grasp this important, encouraging truth?

Sally Michael believes that a child who can embrace God's providence can rest in God's sovereign care, and she uses simple truths to help you explain God's providence to all your children. She moves on to show children how God's providence applies to all of life and creation . . . including themselves.

How many fears, worries, frustrations, and tears would be spared if your children truly understood and rested in the providence of God?

"My heart soars with worship and joy and zeal as I page through Sally's new book, *God's Providence*. . . . Here is a foundation for life that is solid enough to sustain parents and children through the hardest times they will ever face. . . . And here is practical application for children and those who love them enough to teach them."
—**JOHN PIPER,** Author; Associate Pastor for Preaching and Vision, Chancellor, Bethlehem College and Seminary

"Sally Michael has written a primer on God's providence that is richly biblical and theological. This is a helpful resource for parents to introduce their children to God's constant watching and working in our world, and one that provides numerous opportunities for reflection and discussion."
—**BRANDON D. CROWE,** Associate Professor of New Testament, Westminster Theological Seminary

Other Resources from P&R for Growing in God's Wisdom

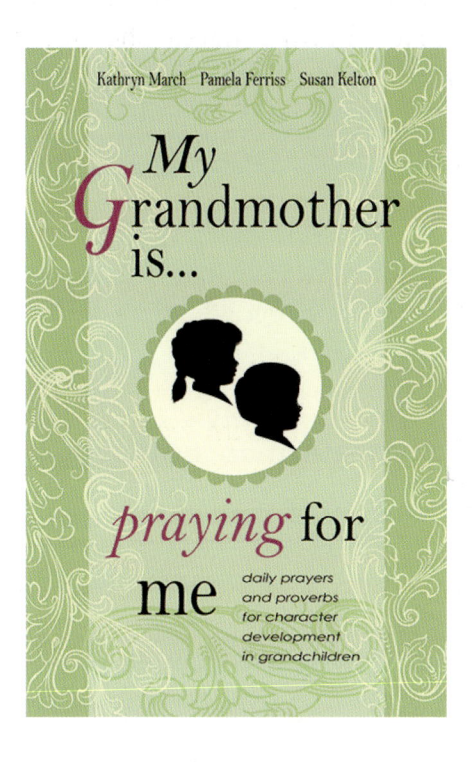

Are you a grandmother? Or maybe you know a grandmother, are married to one, or fondly remember your own. Whatever category you are in, authors and grandmothers Kathryn March, Pamela Ferriss, and Susan Kelton invite you to join them in becoming actively involved in the lives of grandchildren.

The world continues to change, and sometimes it seems that the generation gap has never been larger. But one thing always holds fast: our children and grandchildren need to know and live by the wisdom that God has outlined for them in His Word. Concerned grandparents want their grandchildren to know His Word for themselves—and there is no better way for this to happen than to pray to the Author of all wisdom.

Here is a yearlong, day-by-day guide for grandmothers not only to pray for the godly character development of their grandchildren, but also to teach them to apply His Word to their lives. Each day's entry contains:

- A verse from Proverbs, the book of wisdom
- A prayer specific to the day's verse
- An activity helping grandmothers and grandchildren to interact in a practical application of the verse's truth.

Use the thoughtful prayers of these three concerned grandmothers to guide you as you pray for your own grandchildren, and take comfort in knowing that praying for your grandchildren's growth is a uniquely Christlike thing to do—one that will not fail to bring them nearer to the wisdom of God, Christ himself.

While we all want our grandchildren to know that we are praying for them, it is the first priority of *My Grandmother Is . . . Praying for Me* that grandchildren know God and His promise to hear and answer those who call on Him. May He bless your family as you call on Him for your grandchildren.

Other Resources for Children from P&R

Go to the Ant is a collection of Proverbs in song for the family. God's wisdom can now be musically rooted in hearts and minds through these Scripture-based melodies.

Christian recording artist Judy Rogers, heard worldwide, features adult contemporary, children's, and praise and worship music. All recordings are available from P&R Publishing and Judy Rogers.

"Judy Rogers's music is one of a kind. Biblically concerned parents should obtain her tapes at all cost."
—JAY ADAMS, Author, Speaker, Seminary Professor

"Judy Rogers's music is the music of heaven, weaving together the three great virtues, goodness, truth, and beauty."
—R. C. SPROUL JR., Director, Highlands Study Center

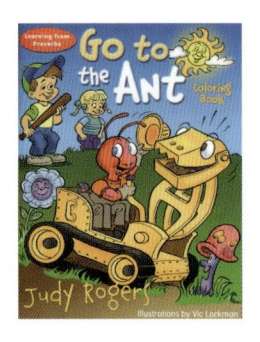

Two coloring books based on *Go to the Ant* are available, too!

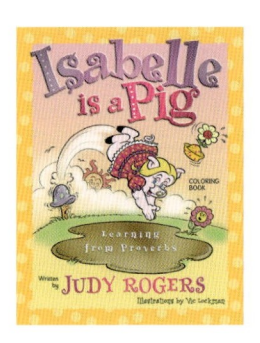

Based on Judy Rogers's song "Isabelle Is a Pig" from her album *Go to the Ant*, this coloring book is a great way to introduce the Proverbs to your children. It will delight and entertain children while teaching them how to be beautiful from the inside out. Judy has added questions to the back of the book that will help parents show that Jesus is the only one who can give them changed hearts and the beauty that counts.